THE
POLITICAL INTEGRATION
OF
URBAN SQUATTERS

NORTHWESTERN
UNIVERSITY
PRESS

African Urban Studies

EDITED BY
REMI CLIGNET AND
EDWARD W. SOJA

MATHARE VALLEY VILLAGE 2, SHOWING THE MAIN ROAD RUNNING THROUGH THE COMMUNITY.

A VILLAGE MEETING IN FRONT OF THE SOCIAL HALL. GITAU IS ADDRESSING THE CROWD WITH A MICROPHONE (FAR RIGHT).

MARC HOWARD ROSS

The political integration of urban squatters

NORTHWESTERN
UNIVERSITY
PRESS

Evanston   1973

Marc Howard Ross is Assistant Professor
of Political Science at Bryn Mawr College.

TO MY PARENTS

Contents

List of figures and tables xi

Preface xiii

1   *Introduction* 3

2   *Community formation* 20

3   *Urban squatters in developing nations* 38

4   *Community organization and political integration
    in squatter settlements* 63

5   *Urban growth and squatters in Nairobi* 82

6   *Political integration in Mathare 2* 97

7   *Sense of community in Mathare 2* 132

8   *Strength of community institutions in Mathare 2* . . . 155

9   *Political integration in local communities* 182

10 *The political integration of urban squatters* 190

Bibliography 210

Index 225

List of figures and tables

Figures

3.1 Developmental Patterns of Squatter Settlements . .   56
6.1 Minutes of the General Village Meeting,
Mathare Village 2, October 9, 1967 101
6.2 Minutes of Village Committee Meeting,
August 22, 1967 104
8.1 Letter to the Honorable Dr. F. M. Waiyaki 177
10.1 Hypothesized Phases in the Community
Formation Process in Mathare 2 199

Tables

6.1 Content Area of Cases Reported to Mathare Elders,
by Degree of Resolution 114
6.2 Measures of Political Integration in Mathare 2 . . . 125
7.1 Comparison of Land Ownership Outside Nairobi
of Mathare Residents and Other Nairobi Africans   134
7.2 Comparison of Education and Occupation of Mathare
Residents with Nairobi Residents, by Sex 136
7.3 Incidence of Beer Brewing, by Sex, among
Mathare Residents 137
7.4 Costs Involved in Brewing and Selling
Millet Beer in Mathare 138
7.5 Participation in Village Political Institutions
in Mathare 2 152
7.6 Summary of Variables Explaining Sense of
Community in Mathare 2 154

List of Figures and Tables

8.1 Comparison of Migration and Urban Experience of
     Mathare Residents and Other Nairobi Africans . . 158
8.2 Comparison of Tribe and Place of Birth of Mathare
     Residents and Other Nairobi Africans 160
8.3 Comparison of Household and Family Structure of
     Mathare Residents and Other Nairobi Africans . . 162
8.4 Comparison of Location of Closest Friends among
     Mathare Residents and Other Nairobi Africans . . 166
8.5 Comparison of Urban Experience and Social Status
     of Leaders and Nonleaders in Mathare 173
8.6 Summary of Variables Explaining Institutional
     Strength in Mathare 2 180
9.1 Summary of Variables Explaining Local-Level
     Integration in Mathare 2 188
10.1 Relative Importance of Variables Accounting
     for Political Integration in Mathare 2 193

Preface

Social change and urbanization are not neutral processes. Rather, the rate, level, and form which they take produce particular hardships or benefits unevenly across individuals, social groups, and societies. At the same time, individuals are not simply victims of social and political situations. They often engage in actions which may sharply alter their environment. Analysis of urban development in Africa, Asia, and Latin America therefore requires both understanding of the situational conditions which define an individual's or group's relative advantage or disadvantage in the society and consideration of how the individual or group responds to that situation.

Urban squatters typically are among the poorest, most disadvantaged elements in the cities of developing nations. They suffer disproportionately from the social change processes in their societies. Nonetheless, in city after city, the squatters' response is neither simply to accept their fate nor to organize their discontent in an effort to destroy the societies in which they are located. More typically, squatter organization, when it develops, is directed inward toward the problems of the squatter settlement itself. The demands which are made on the wider society are limited to seeking basic amenities or freedom from the threat of being bulldozed out of existence. This study tries to explain the success of collective action and community organization in Mathare Valley Village 2, one squatter community in Nairobi, Kenya. It is a community where few outsiders expect to find organization at all, let alone one which is highly successful.

To a social scientist, the challenge of the story of one community, such as Mathare Village 2, is to find and employ concepts which permit the comparison of the community with others in different settings. After deliberation and discussion the concepts

Preface

I chose to use here are those found in the literature on national and international integration. It is important, I believe, that a single case not be viewed as unique, and that case studies should do more than "just present the data" for all to see. The development of empirically based social science theory requires more. At a minimum it means that researchers must, sometimes self-consciously, aim to integrate theory and data, whether they work in one small village or with cross-national data. I have tried here to indicate the steps involved in doing this. Furthermore, I have gone further than the data permit in developing generalizations and hypotheses about the political integration process in an effort to work through the implications for further comparative study of the concepts used in studying a single squatter settlement.

I had no intention of studying urban squatters in Mathare or anywhere else in Kenya when I first arrived in Nairobi in 1967, as is explained in the first chapter. This study is truly inductive in that it developed and increased in intensity the more involved in the community I became, and the more that friends encouraged me in the research. This project would not have been undertaken at all if it had not been for Andrew Hake, then with the Christian Council of Kenya, who first told me about the community and then urged me to study it. Dick Bancroft provided continual support and stimulation as we shared experiences with squatters in Mathare and Langata, where he had close community ties. Mary Jane Patterson and Edward Njenga of the Eastleigh Community Center were important brokers for both the residents of Mathare and myself. During a return visit to Nairobi in 1970, Donna Haldane made available a great deal of material on Mathare in particular, and on squatters in Nairobi in general. Many officials in the Nairobi City Council and the Kenya government answered questions and provided me with information on a number of occasions and always encouraged my research in a setting where little hard data were available.

A number of colleagues and friends have read earlier drafts of this manuscript and provided numerous useful suggestions. Jennie-Keith Ross, my wife, provided invaluable help at every stage of the preparation of the manuscript, from supporting me on her research grant during the writing of the first draft to the substantive suggestions and the proofreading which came later. I owe special thanks to Remi Clignet, Roger Cobb, and Charles Elder, all of whom commented extensively on the manuscript, helping me to develop ways to integrate the theoretical material and the data. In addition, I want to thank Lucy Behrman, L. Gray Cowan, Philip Kilbride, Joan Nelson, Ed Soja, Tom Weisner, Beatrice Whiting, and John Whiting for assistance and comments on various stages of the project, from the field work to final writing. The Council for Intersocietal Studies at Northwestern University provided the funds for the fieldwork.

Lastly, but most importantly, my thanks go to the people of Mathare Village 2 for the warmth and genuine hospitality they showed me during my stay in Nairobi. W. Gitau Gachukia, the village secretary, worked on the project for several months as a research assistant, and without his help in translating village records and in explaining local events this study would not have been possible. Although his two years of secondary school made him a well-educated man when he first came to Nairobi in the early 1940s, Gitau was discarded as unqualified and too old by a society which changed faster than he could. E. W. Kiboro, the head of the village, always had time to talk and drink with me, and provided whatever village records I needed or sought. His openness and trust toward me meant acceptance from most community residents. Furthermore, I want to thank specifically Kariuki Gichohi, my namesake in the community, Gathoni Mbuthia, Kinami, and the many people, most of whose names I never learned, with whom I exchanged greetings and stories almost daily. It is the people of Mathare who made this study an exciting task. Similarly, it is the people of Mathare, and others like them, whom I hope this study will benefit most directly. The people of Mathare are neither looking for handouts nor threatening the social and political order of their society. Instead, they are seeking control over their own lives, and ways to solve the daily problems of subsistence. They reject the negative image that outsiders hold of them and will go to great lengths to alter it, given the opportunity. A better understanding of these aspirations will, I hope, result in a more reasonable and humane government orientation toward urban squatters and greater assistance in helping people to help themselves.

THE
POLITICAL INTEGRATION
OF
URBAN SQUATTERS

1

Introduction

The rapid changes taking place in the developing countries of ·Africa, Asia, and Latin America are seen most vividly in their booming urban centers. While the casual eye may fail to notice widespread alterations in rural life, it cannot help but be struck by the growth and frenzied activity in metropolitan areas, which often double in population every ten years. Such cities represent both the promise and the frustration of social change, and contain within them new social forms and institutions to serve human needs in the urban environment.

Governments and other social agencies can hardly keep up with the pace of change, as the cities lure more and more peasants from the rural areas. Consequently, social planners continually find themselves on a treadmill; the number of jobs and social services never seems to rise as quickly as the number of people seeking them. This is partially because of a shortage of money and partially because demand is conditioned by existing supply; if jobs were to be found for everyone seeking them in most cities, a new wave of migration would be unleashed as people in the rural areas learned that there were urban jobs to be had. In order to cope with the present situation, urban residents have begun to develop new institutions to meet their needs.

One of the most widespread methods of coping is the urban

squatter settlement, found in Africa, Asia, and particularly in Latin America, and known under a variety of names: *barrios, barriadas, villes miserables, favelas,* shanty towns, *bustees,* and *bidonvilles.* Urban squatters are people who live on land which they neither own nor occupy legally and who build their homes without the assistance of government. They usually make up a sizable proportion of the population of most large cities in developing nations, and in some cases constitute more than *half* the urban residents. In 1965 one-quarter of Lima, Peru's, two million residents were squatters (Mangin 1967:68); there were 750,000 in Djakarta (a quarter of the population), 320,000 (23 per cent of the population) in Manila (Dwyer 1964:153); and two million (half the population) in Mexico City (Mangin 1967:68). The spread of squatting is perhaps what John Turner (1969a:107) describes as "a manifestation of normal urban growth processes under historically unprecedented conditions."

Given the millions of squatters and thousands of squatter settlements in the world, it is not surprising that there should be a great deal of variation in the kinds of communities, the forms of internal organization, and the reactions of the wider societies in which the squatters live. Depending on the economic position of the squatters, some settlements are found in the crowded center-city business districts on small open lots, while others are located in the peripheral areas of the city. Some are politically organized communities, while others have no local organization at all. Some squatters work in salaried full-time jobs, while others eke out the barest subsistence through a number of marginal and quasi-legal jobs.

Many questions arise as a result of the range of variation in squatters' communities. What, for example, accounts for the presence or absence of local organization? Why do some communities have local leaders and institutions which not only deal with government officials in trying to obtain security of tenure for the residents but also work to resolve local social and political problems in the settlement? Can these differences be best explained by the relative desperation of some squatters, contradicting the established notion in political behavior literature that social and economic deprivation lead to political apathy (Almond and Verba 1963; Campbell et al. 1960; Milbrath 1965)? Or are they best explained by the relative lack of harassment of squatters from some governments, with the result that the most organized squatters are those who may need organization the least?

There are parallel questions about the factors affecting the process of community formation in urban squatter areas; these are the subject of this book. In part, this is a study of a single squatter community in Nairobi, Kenya. However, to answer these questions about one community, it is also necessary to ask more general questions about the processes of community formation and political integration. Since squatting is a phenomenon occurring in cities throughout the world, it is also appropriate to compare squatter communities in Africa, Asia, and Latin America to note both the general trends and the ways in which developments diverge in different areas.

Mathare Valley Village 2: an introduction

Downtown Nairobi is beautiful, with its tall buildings, modern architecture, and flowering trees. Nairobi is the capital of the recently independent nation of Kenya, and the central area houses the government offices, financial offices, tourist hotels, and curio shops. Four miles from the downtown area, along the sides of the Mathare River valley, live some 10,000 to 20,000 urban squatters (as of 1968). The area, housing four squatter settlements, or "villages," is ugly. The houses, crammed together in an apparently haphazard fashion dictated by the uneven terrain of the valley's walls, are built of mud and wattle and have roofs made of cardboard, flattened-out tin cans, or even sheet metal. A visitor entering the area is struck by the lack of social services; the roads are makeshift, garbage is piled in open areas, and children play in the dust, which is uncontrolled by any vegetation.

The inhabitants of Mathare are generally urban misfits and rural outcasts. They lack the skills necessary to find jobs in the modern economy, while at the same time there are no meaningful rural alternatives to which they can turn. For example, one man fought with the British in Burma in World War II; came back to Nairobi and later joined the Kikuyu Freedom Fighters, who precipitated the declaration of the State of Emergency in Kenya in 1952;[1] was detained for several years; and has not held a permanent job since then. Another worked as a clerk in a law office in Nairobi until a relative of the lawyer became old enough to take over the job. Because he had little education and could not compete with the better-educated young people in Nairobi today, the clerk never found another job. A woman worked in city hall, cleaning the floors every night. She was in a detention camp at the time of Mau Mau and has not had a steady job since then. A younger woman, whose parents died during the Emergency, has two illegitimate children; she has no rights to rural lands and lives in the city by hawking fruits, vegetables, or anything else she can sell.

The squatter in Mathare is highly marginal in every sense of the term. Not only are most of them jobless and landless, but their daily existence is highly insecure because of the constant threat of arrest and harassment resulting from the most important local economic activity, the illegal brewing and selling of *pombe* (locally made beer). Police intervention in Mathare is frequent, and it threatens not only the beer brewers and sellers but almost everyone in the area through their status as squatters, tax evaders, or insecure persons forced to pay protection money.

One of the four settlements, Mathare Valley Village 2, has about 2,000 people living in 700 rooms. (In Mathare, the room is the typical household unit.) The village is long and narrow, running along the hillside for about half a mile, with an average

---

1. The State of Emergency was announced by the colonial government in 1952 in reaction to the so-called Mau-Mau Rebellion.

width of about 100 yards. A single path, wide enough for two cars in most places, runs from the main road at the top of the hill along the length of the village, and is lined by small, sparsely stocked shops. Most rooms are about twelve feet by ten feet, and have at least one wooden window which provides light, a wooden door, and unfinished mud walls. Furniture consists of a bed or two, a table, several chairs and stools, and sometimes a chest.

The most striking aspect of Mathare 2, however, is neither the marginal existence attributable to economic conditions nor the inadequate physical conditions, for while these are not pleasant or necessary, they are frequently found in growing cities throughout the world. What is so striking about the community is that it is highly organized and politically integrated, apparently in response to the particular set of conditions facing the residents. There is a clearly identifiable group of community leaders who direct the village committee, a Kenya African National Union (KANU) branch, a committee of elders who act as a judicial body, a cooperative society based in the village, and a youth wing which serves as the village police. The village maintains several "nursery schools," which take care of children between four and eight or nine years of age who are unable to attend government schools (usually for lack of money); holds adult education classes; organizes community work projects; and runs a social hall in the center of the village.

The social hall is the only building in the village with electricity. This comes from a small generator that the village leaders purchased, and it supplies power for the electric guitars which are owned by the village and used at the nightly dances. Proceeds from the dances and from the sale of beer and other refreshments in the social hall yield a very small income for some members of the community and finance village projects such as the expansion of the nursery school. Most important, however, the proceeds provide money to help pay the fines of villagers arrested for illegal beer brewing or possession, the bribes paid to police, and the entertainment of important visitors to the village, such as politicians, government officials, or high-ranking police officers.

Sociologically, it is no longer very striking to assert that slums or squatter communities are not necessarily zones of social disorganization. Mathare 2, however, represents more than a case of a physically marginal area with an identifiable social or political organization. Unlike virtually all other neighborhoods in Nairobi, there is a relatively well-developed sense of community and a series of effective local political and social institutions which provide for the peaceful resolution of local problems. Why this is so is a question that fascinated me from the first day that I visited the village, and is the central question of this book.

Logic of discovery

I first went to Mathare in September, 1967, while doing research in several other neighborhoods of Nairobi. Because so little material existed which described the social or political life among the African population of the city, I considered it important to visit as many different neighborhoods as possible. Andrew Hake, then working with the Christian Council of Kenya, had told me about Mathare, and the extent of political organization there. He put me in contact with Mary Jane Patterson, an American working at the nearby Eastleigh Community Center, who knew the leaders and a number of people from the village.

That first day we sat around visiting and talking with people in different parts of the village. The village secretary, W. Gitau Gachukia, asked me if I knew anything about bookkeeping. He explained that, according to government regulations, the cooperative society was supposed to file a monthly report with the Ministry of Cooperatives. However, after eighteen months, they still had not filed their first report, and the government was threatening to revoke their license. I agreed to return a few days later to see if I could help. For the most part, the task was relatively simple; the books were in good order, and all that had to be done was to prepare a balance sheet describing the state of affairs of the cooperative at that time. After that was finished, the leader of the village, E. W. Kiboro, asked me to help organize the accounts for the social hall, which I agreed to do.

Throughout this time I had no intention of conducting research in Mathare, although I was becoming more and more interested in the complex operation of the community's institutions. For one thing, the records indicated that over 90 members of the cooperative had paid almost 7,000 shillings in shares, and over 300 people had paid more than 12,000 shillings into the social hall, all this in a relatively short time. When I began to ask questions about the community institutions, the responses were fascinating. Most of the leaders were former freedom fighters, and a majority of the twenty-two members of the village committee had been placed in British detention camps during Mau Mau. Some had lived in Mathare before the Emergency. When I asked what exactly the village committee did, Gitau showed me a binder containing the minutes of all their meetings, which he had typed—in duplicate!

Soon the temptation became irresistible. I told the village committee that I was interested in writing a history of the community and in describing the self-help efforts and political organization of Mathare Valley Village 2. They told me I could conduct my research and interview people in the community on two conditions: I had to interview the members of the committee before interviewing anyone else, and I had to give them a copy of whatever I wrote. I agreed to both conditions, and, proceeding in an inductive manner, I began to learn all I could about the political organization and activity of the village. I spent hours in the village office and walking around talking to people; I went to committee meetings as well as to general village meetings to see what went on there; I continued to help with the accounting and bookkeeping; and I reviewed all the village records—financial statements, committee minutes, and cases heard by the elders.

At the same time I became more and more involved as a participant, and developed a role in the community's institutional structure. Kibro began to ask me to speak at the village *baraza* (meeting). At first he was content to have me state vaguely that I was very impressed with the leaders and organizations in the village. Soon after, however, he wanted me to be more specific—for example, he insisted that I tell the people that a report had been prepared for the Ministry of Cooperatives and that the records of the cooperative society had showed that the books were in order and there was no mismanagement. On other occasions, when the leaders were collecting money for village projects, I was asked to sit with them and was placed in charge of writing receipts. The effect of this and similar actions increasingly identified me with the village leadership, which minimized my ability to study political conflicts *within* the community and tended to increase the status and legitimacy of the leaders.[2]

At this time, the official policy of both the Kenya and the Nairobi government toward Mathare might be described as one of "negative nonrecognition," which meant that despite the fact that people living in Mathare paid taxes, the community received no government services. For example, the villagers raised enough money to install a water pipe running from the center of the village to the road at the top of the hill. They then asked the city to install a water meter and *sell* them water. The answer was a refusal. In effect the government said, "You are illegal

2. One of the most important skills of the leaders, particularly Kiboro, is the ability to use knowledge of Nairobi politics in acting as a broker between the villagers and the government. My presence in the village was further evidence of this. My positive statements concerning the financial records were used to counter continual rumors that there was mismanagement of funds. Not only was I an outsider testifying that the leaders were honest, but I was also a "European," a fact which is still important in post-independence Kenya.

squatters, therefore you have no right to buy clean water."

The attitude was widespread, and not only among government officials, that Mathare was a "den of thieves" and a dirty place which needed to be eradicated. Along with Andrew Hake, I sought to influence people in the city planning department, the city council, and other government departments by providing more complete information (both statistical and descriptive) about Mathare, in an effort to affect future government policy. For example, we presented one paper to a conference concerned with urban problems in Africa, where we argued that urban planners must be more sensitive to the use of local authority structures in achieving long-range goals and discussed programs that might be considered for a community such as Mathare. At the same time, when speaking to officials it was necessary to avoid an "open confrontation," because we feared that if officials felt trapped and were publicly forced to choose between "standards" and squatters, the entire community might be bull-dozed.

The problem is very sensitive because of the desire on the part of Kenya's elite to show that they can manage a city such as Nairobi as effectively as did the British colonial administration. The growth of squatter communities, which did not exist under the British, makes the administrators susceptible to charges of incompetence. The presence of unrealistic building codes, dating from colonial rule, which make houses constructed of traditional materials illegal in most of the city, poses a second problem to planners and administrators. If, for example, they change the codes, they are afraid of being accused of "lowering standards" and permitting Africans to live under conditions that are unsuitable for Europeans.

The danger to the community of directly challenging the authorities in public is clearly shown in the story of a police raid on the village which followed an article in one of the Nairobi newspapers about the community's self-help activities. A reporter from the *Daily Nation* heard about the activities of the village leaders, spent an afternoon in the village (where the leaders say they treated him coldly, because they thought that he was sent to make trouble by political opponents of the Member of Parliament [M.P.] for the area), and then wrote a very favorable article about the village's organization and needs. The police, meanwhile, were placed in a difficult position because the article had outlined the importance of illegal beer brewing to the villagers. That night, they raided the social hall for the first time in almost a year (it had not been subject to raids by mutual agreement between the police and the village leaders), arrested over seventy people, and fined the villagers over Shs. 2800/-, which the leader paid the next morning.

The logic of inquiry

Through participant observation, analysis of records, interviews with government officials, and an interview schedule administered to a sample of the residents of Mathare 2, a great deal of data about politics and social life in the community were obtained. Because of the inductive nature of the research, data collection was not organized on the basis of a well-articulated set of hypotheses and a set of interrelated variables. The approach was much more ad hoc; any data that might better explain the nature of the political organization in the village and its apparent success were pursued.

In first searching for a concept that might organize the study, I believed that I was studying legitimacy. For example, I wondered why some 75 per cent of the homeowners in the village contributed ten shillings each to a fund for improving the water supply, when at the same time most sought to avoid payment of any taxes to the Kenya government. (One possible explanation, that of coercion and intimidation within the village, was ruled out on the basis of observation.) Gradually, I decided that legitimacy was an important concept that had to be considered, but that it was not sufficiently general to provide the basis for the study.

More and more I began to conceptualize the study in terms of the idea of community, referring to such processes as the development of a "sense of community" and community formation. None seemed exactly appropriate, because so much of the literature about small communities in Africa is based on studies of traditional communities, where the participants have been in face-to-face contact with one another for their entire lives (not to mention the ancestral ties that come into play in social life), rather than for under five years, as is the case in Mathare. On the other hand, to the extent that community studies have been concerned with the identification of members with a community and the workings of community-wide institutions, I was interested in these writings.

There is one body of literature, however, that is concerned with questions of community identification from the perspective of community formation. Unlike local community studies, studies of national and international integration usually consider directly the process of community formation—the development of identification with a particular community and the growth and spread of community-wide institutions. Studies of nation-building or international integration are much more common in Africa (and other areas also) than are studies of local community formation. However, as the theoretical content of my question concerning the extent and effectiveness of Mathare's institutions seemed closest to questions posed in the political integration literature, I decided to use these questions to organize the material. At the same time, I hoped to learn more about the process of political integration by studying integration on a different level than did most previous studies.

A second way to understand what is happening in Mathare is to look at the urbanization process in developing nations. Most cities have housing for hundreds of thousands of squatters. Furthermore, studies show that many of the popular stereotypes about urban squatters are exaggerations or are totally unsupported by the facts. For example, although squatters tend to be migrants to the city, most cases where data is available show that they are not the most recent immigrants; usually they have at least five or six years of urban experience.

Mathare 2 is, in many ways, a product of the rapid urbanization and social change taking place in the developing nations. Particularly in Africa, where urban growth rates have not yet begun to level off, it appears that the form of social and political organization found in Mathare will have an increased importance in the coming decades. Thus to understand Mathare it is useful to look at both the urbanization process in developing nations and the squatter phenomenon.

Mathare and the wider society

The picture I developed of Mathare 2 was one of a small, relatively cohesive community with a wide variety of institutions handling local problems ranging from education and dispute settlement to the regulation of illegally brewed beverages. At the same time, in many ways the community is dependent on the wider society and hardly autonomous in the ways that rural communities can be. For one thing, the customers for the beer and other services come from outside Mathare. The location of the community near an air force base, a police barracks, a mental hospital, and the neighborhood of Eastleigh is important economically, as the beer trade is highly location-specific.

Since Mathare 2 is an urban neighborhood in the country's capital city, both city and national politics have an impact on the community. Politics in Kenya has moved from mass-based party politics, which encouraged widespread participation in the electoral system, to more individualistic, privatized elite involvement in the few years between independence in 1963 and the late 1960s when this study of Mathare took place (Ross 1973). High social class and status are becoming prerequisites for political involvement, as the gap between the elite and the masses has steadily increased (Ross forthcoming). At the same time, ethnicity and tribal differences are more and more important in shaping orientations toward the government and in the politics of resource allocation (Ross forthcoming: chaps. 8, 9). In particular, politics is controlled largely by the Kikuyu, the country's largest tribe, and their allies, while groups in western Kenya, such as the Luo, and coastal groups are more and more estranged from the government. The latter groups feel that the criteria for resource allocation are increasingly based on ethnic and kinship considerations (Ross forthcoming:chap. 8).

The increased emphasis on both class and ethnic factors in Kenya politics in the period following independence has led to the growth of what Gordon (1964) calls an "ethclass," made up mainly of wealthy Kikuyu, who hold the most powerful political positions in both the city and the country. Their emphasis has been on maintaining and expanding the structure of the economic system inherited from the British, rather than on altering priorities and changing the pattern of incipient peasant capitalism (Leys 1971:310).[3]

Although the Kikuyu recognized the importance of creating a broad-based coalition to rule Kenya during the independence period, by 1970 they were far more determined to dominate any political grouping and were reluctant to share political power equally.[4]

3. Leys argues quite convincingly that peasant-based clientship politics, as opposed to a truly class-based division, is likely to dominate the Kenya political scene for some time. He does not, I believe, spell out carefully enough the importance of ethnic and regional differences, although he clearly does mention them. In a sense, what has developed in Kenya is a stratification system based on both class and ethnicity; that is, the elite of two ethnic groups, such as the Kikuyu and the Luo, are antagonistic, and the gap between the elite and the mass in any single ethnic group is also marked.

4. By 1970, following the assassination of Tom Mboya and the widespread oath-taking among the Kikuyu, ethnic relations in Kenya grew markedly worse as suspicion and distrust rose sharply. Increasingly, the Kikuyu did not want to share power, and an increasing number said that they deserved to be in control because they "had done most of the fighting and suffering in the fight for independence." Thus their current rewards are considered payment for past suffering. This is also seen in the increased sentiment for making Kikuyu, rather than Swahili or English, the national language, and in the increased feeling

The special meaning of the Mau Mau period for the Kikuyu still has a tremendous influence on Kenya politics. For some it is still a symbol of Kikuyu courage and an indicator that they were the only group who "stood up to the British." For others its memory lies more in the social dislocation it caused. Essentially a civil war between Kikuyu factions (Rosberg and Nottingham 1966), the period ended with the breakup of families, thousands of deaths, and the reallocation of a good deal of land in Central Province (Sorrenson 1967; Harbeson 1971). Many of the "losers" drifted off to the cities and towns in the early 1960s, and a sizable proportion of the squatter population today is, in effect, the residue of the domestic turmoil of that earlier period. It would be a mistake, however, to see the squatters as a landless, urbanized proletariat, ripe for radicalization. In fact, they are among the strongest supporters of the present government despite the fact that it has done little or nothing to improve their lives.[5]

While many of the squatters expressed keen disappointment that they had not received land in one of the settlement schemes in the White Highlands, and were openly critical of the lack of government assistance in improving their living conditions, they did not see these matters as the fault of President Jomo Kenyatta and other prominent Kikuyu politicians.[6] In fact, unlike

---

that Nairobi is a Kikuyu city and that other groups are temporary visitors or outsiders. Another marker of Kikuyu ethnicity increasingly common in Nairobi in 1970 was a proliferation of pictures of Dedan Kimanthi, a leader of the freedom fighters who was killed by the British after his capture in 1955. These pictures are hung inside Kikuyu homes alongside pictures of President Kenyatta.

5. This situation is common in a wide range of urban situations; outside observers who assume that social deprivation and frustration will result in political radicalization are frequently proved wrong. After reviewing a wide range of relevant data, Nelson (1969:67) concludes that "the bulk of economic and social frustration is likely to leak into alternative channels, including non-radical political action."

6. While he was still alive, many Kikuyu in Nairobi blamed the failures of the government on Minister for Economic Development and Planning Tom Mboya, a Luo, while attributing the successes to Kenyatta or other Kikuyus.

many other poor groups in Nairobi, the Mathare squatters appeared to be satisfied with the symbolic reassurance provided by frequent reminders that indeed Africans, and particularly Kikuyus, are now heading their government (Edelman 1964). Their expectations are not high. They accept the basic legitimacy of a stratified social system in which the majority of the rewards go to the highly educated few. Rather than seeking to destroy this elite group, they want their children to become part of it. Most important, their ethnic identification proves to be their primary attachment and the basis for their political mobilization (Edelman 1971). In 1969, KANU began administering long ritual oaths which stressed loyalty to President Kenyatta and Kikuyu solidarity, and the people of Mathare were among the first to appear at Kenyatta's rural home at Gatundu to pay their ten shillings and take the oath.

To a great extent the reluctance of the squatters to see their social situation as having roots in Kenya's politics and social structure seems to have encouraged them to turn inward in seeking to solve the problems of subsistence and conflict management they face in their daily lives. While hoping that the government will eventually decide to assist them in their effort to find a permanent plot of land, they do not believe that they will have a personal impact on such a decision. In this sense they feel powerless to affect government policy and fatalistic about the future. Their major concerns are more immediate and personal. Life is better than it was under the colonial government, but not as good as it could be.

This study focuses primarily on the squatters themselves, rather than seeking to uncover the roots of the *laissez faire* government attitude. It is based on developments in the community through March, 1968, although a few comments are made

---

Mboya, originally elected in a largely Kikuyu constituency, in effect served as the lightning rod for Kikuyu dissent, and his political popularity fell sharply before his death.

concerning later developments noticed during a brief return visit in 1970. The inquiry asks what the factors are which help account for the community formation process in Mathare 2 at a time when the government was essentially uninterested in providing any assistance, and when the dominant public attitude toward urban squatters in Kenya was that they should "go back to the land." Since the time of the study, there have been significant changes in the attitudes and politics of the Nairobi and Kenya governments toward squatters, and these are discussed below. The major question here, however, is how to account for the creation of community sentiments and institutions in Mathare 2, and we are interested in understanding the attitudes and actions of outsiders primarily as they directly help to answer this question.

Plan of the book

We begin by studying a single community, Mathare Valley Village 2, a squatter community in a rapidly developing city, to discover how we can account for its high level of political organization. As we proceed inductively, two different bodies of literature seem most useful in helping to answer this question. The first is the literature of community formation and political integration, which provides a theoretical context for our inquiry. The second is the literature concerned with urbanization and squatter communities in developing countries, which locates Mathare in a physical setting increasingly common in Africa, Asia, and Latin America.

Chapter 2 examines the concepts of community and political integration by focusing on two components: an attitudinal element (sense of community) and a behavioral component (the development of community institutions). Chapters 3 and 4 link the study of political integration to studies of urban squatter settlements, first outlining major causes of urban growth in developing nations, then reviewing the major elements of social and political organization in urban squatter settlements, and finally developing eleven hypotheses which seem to account for political integration in these communities. These hypotheses are used in Chapters 5 through 9 to help account for the level of political integration in Mathare 2. Finally, Chapter 10 ranks the previously discussed variables in terms of their relative contribution to the integration process in Mathare 2, proposes a model for interrelating the variables, and suggests particular stages associated with the community formation process in Mathare 2. Our hope is that the theoretical orientation will help place Mathare 2 in a more general context, and that at the same time the insights gained from Mathare 2 can contribute to the development of political integration theory.

2

Community formation

Political communities are created in a variety of settings, as men work together to achieve goals and accomplish tasks they are unable to manage alone. On the local level, individuals or families move into a new area and develop social and political institutions, drawing on their past experiences and future aspirations. On the national level, once-artificial states drawn by the colonial map makers of Europe are creating national identities and institutions to serve their citizens, who are beginning to feel they are members of a state their grandparents never heard of. On the international level, formerly sovereign nations are slowly relinquishing some of their powers, such as control over the flow of goods and services across their borders, and are forming new communities designed to bring their citizens together rather than to divide them.

Some community formation efforts are the result of the planning and work of individuals, who start with a clear vision of the community they want to create; other communities seem to result from a natural, unplanned flow of events. Some of the best examples of the first type are the utopian communities found throughout the world. Although these communities do not always operate as their founders intended, their plans are usually quite explicit. The second type, relatively unplanned new communities, are well represented by new suburbs or urban neighborhoods built to accommodate the swelling populations of big cities. These are often constructed by building contractors to meet the demand for housing, with very little thought given to the kind of community being created and the sort of social or political institutions appropriate for it.

In either case, important questions arise about the process by which a political community is formed. How do relatively unattached individuals living in one place come to see themselves as having a common fate and requiring either formal or informal institutions to serve their common interests? In Mathare 2, individuals moved into the area in the early 1960s looking for shelter and the opportunity to earn a subsistence income. Five years later one could observe in the community a sense of identity and a wide range of political and social institutions. It is hoped that an examination of this single case can increase our understanding of the process of community formation and, conversely, that concepts pertaining to the community formation process in general can shed light on specific events in Mathare 2.

The concepts of community and political integration are applicable to a wide range of settings and to areas which vary greatly in size, patterns of interaction, or degree of institutionalization. Mathare 2 is similar to many communities studied by anthropologists and sociologists interested in rural areas in that it is a small, homogeneous community. On the other hand, its lack of autonomy and its newness make this village comparable in many ways to the kinds of communities that might be studied by political scientists interested in national or international integration. Because the concepts of community and political integration are not associated with any single level of social organization, one can, in effect, draw on studies at all levels to develop hypotheses concerning the nature of community integration at the local level. Similarly, despite the facts that Mathare is neither as isolated nor as autonomous as most small rural communities and that the individuals in the community have only the most general sense of a common historical past, studies of local rural communities can provide additional hypotheses to help explain the community formation process.

The concept of community

Sociologist Robert Nisbet suggests that everyone wants to talk about community because no one is a member of one any more (1962). Nisbet, like many others, maintains an image of the preindustrial rural community as somehow more "real" than any community found in an urban neighborhood in a contemporary industrial setting. This unfortunate and unrealistic romanticism has hindered our understanding of what a community is. The concept of community can explain contemporary phenomena only if it is applied to empirical reality. Existing communities need to be distinguished, and an understanding must be developed of the consequences of their differences.

Community is not an all or nothing property, either possessed or lacked by a political unit. Rather, it is a continuous variable, whose over-all level is determined by four characteristics that can be present or absent in varying degrees:

1. the association of a particular geographic area with the community;

2. the identification of the territory by its inhabitants as socially or politically distinct;

3. the existence within the territory of a regular and identifiable pattern of social relations and institutions; and

4. a generalized purpose rather than a single specific goal.

While the idea of community refers to an identifiable territorial unit, not all specific geographic areas are communities. For example, no one talks about the community of Antarctica, the Gobi desert community, or even the Middle East community (including both Israel and the United Arab Republic). On the other hand, "community" is sometimes used in reference to a nongeographical unit, such as a professional association or a group of individuals with a common interest (e.g., the scholarly community). For the most part, such uses refer to purposive, situationally specific groups. These groups should achieve increasing importance in social and political life as men travel about the earth and through space, becoming less tied to specific territories. However, rather than calling them communities on an a priori basis (except in a metaphorical way), it would be useful to learn what differences might be attributed to the absence of any territorial orientation.

A second use of "community" that is seemingly without a territorial reference appears when one speaks of a racial or religious community, such as the Hindu community or the black community. While territory is not especially important in its identification, this sort of community is almost always associated with a definite geographical area (often noncontiguous) which is identifiable if necessary. For such communities, however, the presence of a large number of institutions which help to maintain a high level of interaction between members and the lack of specific purposive goals are more important characteristics.

Individuals living in a territory may identify it as socially or politically distinct without necessarily implying their approval or support. For example, enslaved or colonial populations often acknowledge the existence of the community in which they are living although they are not positively oriented toward it. What is important is that individuals perceive that the political and social organization within certain territorial boundaries is distinct from parallel organization beyond these boundaries. In some in-between situations the territory has more a psychological than a political reality. People fighting a colonial power for freedom may have the image of a national community that does not yet exist. Another example is that of the state of Israel, which many Jews held to be an entity before its political creation in 1948.

23

The continent of Africa seems to be regarded similarly by many black Americans today.

Not all communities have the same importance in the lives of their participants, measured either by the proportion of their lives that are spent within the community or by their dependence on the community's institutions and services. The community is probably more important to its participants in the traditional folk society than it is in the urban neighborhood. We expect that the higher the degree of participation, the greater the psychological identification with the community and its institutions (Greer and Minar 1969:ix; Frankenberg 1966:15; and Hillery 1968:3). One possible hypothesis is that identification varies with the extent to which participants see their own welfare and security as coinciding with that of the community.

A community contains within it institutions which contribute to a more or less regular and identifiable pattern of social relations. Through interaction there is a division of labor and the development of interdependence, both of which vary in importance from community to community. The absence of institutions and a low level of interaction in an area indicate that there is a low level of community. Cooperation patterns also vary. In the typical folk society, mutual assistance is characteristic of economic and other activities in the village, while cooperation in cities is organized more often through the division of labor or through contracts. Family and kinship are more important in the social organization of folk communities, although they are not overlooked in urban settings, especially in organizing personal contacts and leisure activities (Hillery 1968:chap. 4; Young and Willmott 1957).

Finally, community means that shared institutions exist independently of specific defining goals. In discussing how communal organizations differ from other forms of organization, Hillery says:

The reasons for living together are often no more than that of being born in the locality (for all communal organizations occupy a particular territory). And though specific reasons draw people to some communal organizations, the people always engage in activities unrelated to the initial attraction. Thus, the migrant may enter a city specifically for a job, but he also marries, plays, goes to church, etc. (1968:186)

Communities are not purposive organizations in the way that business corporations or universities are. The members of a community, if they were asked, would only be able to identify a wide range of general community purposes, and even these are not perceived as very important by community participants on a day-to-day basis. The goals of General Motors or of a supermarket are much more identifiable than those of the city of Nairobi or the nation of Ghana. The latter two are communities, while the first two are not.[1]

The four characteristics discussed above are variables which combine in different ways to determine whether an area should be considered a strong or a weak community. Thus, the more identifiable the geographic area, the more that individuals perceive the territory as distinct, the more institutionalized and regularized the pattern of social relations, and the more general its purposes, the higher the level of community. Using these criteria, social or political units can be placed on a continuum which ranges from the strongest possible community on one end to the complete absence of community on the other. A point somewhere between the two ends of such a continuum could indicate the minimum level below which one can say that a community does not exist; the exact location of this point, however, is somewhat arbitrary, depending in part on the purposes for which it is selected.

Communities defined in this manner can exist in a wide vari-

1. In some ways utopian communities violate this assumption in that they tend to be purposive, at least at the outset. Such a community is still not purposive in the way that a corporation is, however, in that the former has many purposes which tend to be quite general.

ety of situations. Redfield, for example, in his study of "little communities," in which he focused on distinctive, small, homogeneous, and self-sufficient rural communities, notes that there are also little communities in other settings—in urban areas, along the frontier, or even in labor camps (1960:5). Some, such as the rural communities Redfield studies, are likely to be highly isolated and to have a long tradition. On the other hand, a community such as Levittown, New Jersey, a newly developed suburb of Philadelphia, lacks these characteristics. Built in a few short years on previously vacant land, Levittown had few residents who worked in the community. Furthermore, while the builder and local government officials made provision for some of the community's institutions, such as the schools and the police force, most of the social and political organization grew out of the interaction patterns among the residents after their arrival (Gans 1967).

Not all new communities lack autonomy. A striking example is utopian agricultural settlements. Spiro's study of one kibbutz showed the community formation process, beginning with the aspirations and plans of its founders in Europe and ending with an examination of the workability of their ideas forty years later. Although not entirely isolated from outside influences, the daily life on the kibbutz is relatively self-contained. Because of the particular nature of Israel's nation-building effort, the kibbutz, unlike many small rural communities, is able to bring new adult members into the community with relative ease (Spiro 1963).

Communities are not necessarily mutually exclusive, and an individual can participate in more than one community at the same time. For example, most Africans are simultaneously members of their village, tribal, and national communities without finding these memberships incompatible with one another (Guetzkow 1955). Membership in each community at a higher level generally subsumes membership in each of the lower-level communities (Hillery 1968). This is not always true, of course, and the exceptions only serve to highlight the general pattern.

One case is found in Nigeria, where many individuals felt that membership in the Ibo tribal community was incompatible with participation in the Nigerian community during the time of Biafra's existence.

Geographical mobility has also increased the likelihood that individuals will participate in several different communities. During the course of a normal day, a person may sleep in one community, work in another, and market in a third.[2]

Political integration

Political integration is the process whereby formerly independent units (individuals, groups, nations) come together to form new political communities. Examples of integration are seen in the rural settlement schemes in Africa (Chambers 1969), in the suburbs of urban areas (Gans 1967), in new nations (Johnson 1970), and in new supranational organizations (Haas 1964; Lindberg 1963). Integration, like community, can be present in varying degrees. Rather than simply talking about the presence or absence of integration, Jacob and Teune suggest, "It might be more useful to envisage a set of relationships, which are *more* or *less* integrated, or a progression of events leading to an *increase* or a *decrease* in integration" (1964:7).

The definition of political integration used here is taken from a study of international integration which seems equally relevant in considering communities of other levels, sizes, and degrees of autonomy:

> By *integration* we mean the attainment, within a territory, of a "sense of community" and of institutions and practices strong enough and widespread enough to assure, for a "long" time,

2. For some purposes one might want to consider this situation as involving three different communities, while for others it is more useful to see it as involving one larger community. Thus, the question of community boundaries can depend on the purpose one has in mind.

dependable expectations of "peaceful change" among its population.

> By *sense of community* we mean a belief on the part of individuals in a group that they have come to agreement on at least this one point: that common social problems must and can be resolved by processes of "peaceful change."

> By *peaceful change* we mean that resolution of social problems, normally by institutionalized procedures, without resort to large-scale physical force. (Deutsch et al. 1957:5)

The level of integration, according to this definition, is a function of the sense of community in an area and of the institutions and practices associated with conflict resolution and expectations of peaceful change, or the orderly management of political and social problems.[3] In addition, there should be an interaction between these two elements. The presence of a strong sense of community should help to strengthen institutions and, conversely, strong and effective institutions should lead to the development of stronger feelings of community among a population.

Sense of community

Sense of community, the first element in the definition of integration, is the "we feeling"—the loyalty, the sharing of interests, and the trust—that develops within an area. Deutsch and his associates describe it as:

> a "we-feeling," trust, and mutual consideration; of partial identification in terms of self-images and interests; of mutually successful predictions of behavior, and of cooperative action in accordance

3. Some debate exists about whether "integration" should be used to refer to a condition or to a process. When talking about community the distinction is easily made between community (condition) and community formation (process). The integration vocabulary is not so clear, and there is a danger in confusing a measure of one for the other—for example, using the level of transactions between two units as an indicator of the integration process and then using the *same* measure to indicate its level.

with it—in short, a matter of a perpetual dynamic process of
mutual attention, communication, perception of needs, and
responsiveness in the process of decision-making. (1966:17)

It is more than a simple sharing of common values or proposi-
tions, they contend, for there are cases of disintegration (for
example, between the English and the Irish) where there was
a sharing of many values, but where there was little trust, or
"we-feeling," in the community (Deutsch 1966:17-18).

The presence of a strong sense of community means that
people develop a common bond with other community members,
see their lives as interdependent, and consider problems and
solutions within the community as distinctive. In other words,
they believe to some extent that what is good for the community
is good for themselves (at least in the long run). Therefore,
people are willing to accept short-run losses, such as paying
taxes or abiding by a judicial opinion against themselves, without
violent protest. The sense of community is the value component
of legitimacy. It represents the degree to which people in a
community perceive that they share a common fate and therefore
are willing to participate in community institutions, accept community decisions as binding, and support community leaders
in their role as leaders (although at the same time they may
dislike them personally and seek to replace them with an alternative group of leaders).

The sense of community that participants feel, or their degree
of community identification, can be analyzed in terms of their
orientations toward: (1) the community itself—who is included
in the community and what its boundaries are; (2) the regime,
or the system of institutional arrangements in the community;
and (3) the authorities, or the individuals in positions of power
and influence in the community (Easton 1964:chaps. 11-13). Nor-
mally, strong positive feelings directed toward one or two of
these elements should lead to the strengthening of feelings
toward the others, although this is not always the case. In France,

while there has been a strong sense of identification with the nation as a political community, and little debate concerning who is included in the community, this has not spilled over into widespread support for French political institutions or authorities. Given this institutional weakness and the lack of support for most political leaders, it is in some ways only because of strong feelings of community that France has not divided into smaller political units. Communities which have very strong support directed toward the community and regime levels can often tolerate relatively high levels of conflict concerning the authorities, provided this conflict is channeled through the existing institutional structure. Thus bitterly contested elections that are decided by just a few percentage points, which are evidence of high levels of disagreement concerning the authorities, are not necessarily indicative of a weak and fragmented community (Easton 1964).

The political instability of national governments in post-independence Africa can be analyzed in terms of the poorly developed sense of community—the low level of support directed toward the political community, the regime, and the authorities—in a number of nations. Frequently, opposition to a group of leaders is transformed in a short time into opposition to the regime; this finally results in disagreement over the nature of the political community, with members of one or more tribes suggesting that they would be better off if they were to form their own nation. What is observed is the spillover process mentioned above, but instead of the positive feelings for the community being transformed into acceptance of the regime and the authorities, the strong, and more specific, negative feelings toward certain authorities are generalized into negative feelings about the regime and the community. This process often is hastened by political leaders who equate opposition to themselves or their governments with opposition to the nation, thus making it impossible to oppose them as leaders without being accused of treason.

In contrast, there is a strong impression in most local community studies in Africa that there is widespread support directed toward the community, the regime, and the authorities. The legitimacy accorded to traditional systems is high, and where serious conflicts do exist, they most often take the form of competition between rival groups of possible authorities, rather than challenges to the community's basic institutions and practices. This does not necessarily mean, however, that there is little conflict; rather, it means that conflict is dealt with through the existing set of social and political institutions. Evans-Pritchard (1968), for example, shows how the principle of "segmentary opposition" can explain patterns of conflict and conflict management among the Nuer in the Southern Sudan. A Nuer who becomes involved in a social conflict knows whom he can turn to for assistance, where his opponent will seek support, what mechanisms may be used for playing out the conflict, and, finally, what procedures will "finalize" the conflict or bring it to a permanent end so that it does not create an enduring cleavage within the community. The more locally based the conflict, the greater the likelihood that forces will come into play to moderate it and that third-party decisions will be respected by both sides, thereby permitting everyone involved to regard it as finished and to avoid a permanent split in the community. The playing out of conflicts within the boundaries of traditionally prescribed norms and institutions may even help to integrate local communities by providing a public arena for the reaffirmation of community values and loyalties (Gluckman 1966).

Some people have expressed the hope that the relatively high level of legitimacy of traditional communities, regimes, and authorities could be transferred to new, larger communities, particularly nations, in Africa. During the colonial period, for example, local traditional leaders were often made the governmental representatives (variously called local government officials, local chiefs, and so on) and were made responsible for various tasks, most particularly tax collection. However, the result in many cases was that instead of increasing acceptance and support for the colonial government, this practice lowered the influence and legitimacy of the traditional leader. Fallers (1955) shows that there often was an extremely high rate of turnover in government-appointed chiefs because the two roles—traditional leader and government official—created a strain due to contrary expectations of behavior. At the same time that the chiefs were often unsuccessful in the eyes of the government, they were also considered failures by the African population.

Traditional leaders who were installed in power in new social environments, such as cities or industrial settings, were also often unsuccessful. Workers on the Copperbelt in Northern Rhodesia (now Zambia) rejected a system of representation through tribal elders in favor of a union (Epstein 1958). They felt that the colonial authorities and mine managers were able to coopt elders who did not adequately represent their interests. For one thing, in comparison with the alternative union leaders, the traditional elders did not have the skills and abilities needed to operate in an industrial, as opposed to a traditional, setting. While the traditional elders could continue to be respected on the Copperbelt, and to be consulted on such issues as marital disputes, with their advice accepted by both sides, they were not accepted as leaders in all situations. Their authority was limited to matters where their traditional wisdom was considered useful. Thus on the Copperbelt, and in similar cases in other urban settings, the legitimacy of the traditional elders failed to help develop an acceptance of colonial institutions. At the same time, the development of an intertribal labor union to represent the miners who previously had been organized on a tribal basis is evidence of an increasing sense of community among the Africans, which later served in many cases as the basis of the political independence movement. In the rejection of one form of community (that of tribal organization supported by the colonial administration), the miners supported a broader idea of community encompassing all Africans, which they perceived would better serve their urban-based interests.[4]

Institutions and practices

The second element in Deutsch's definition of integration concerns the development in a community of certain institutions and practices that are expected to provide regularized, peaceful management of community problems. Two characteristics of these institutions and practices seem particularly important to community integration: (1) the extent of the tasks performed by community institutions, and (2) their perceived effectiveness.

In some communities, the institutions have a relatively light task load, meaning that the number of tasks the community institutions assume, the number of people affected, and the effect on people's lives are relatively low. This is particularly apt to be true of communities such as urban neighborhoods or suburbs near large urban areas. Rural communities in which the residents are widely dispersed over a large area, and in which they have a low level of interaction, are also likely to have a low task load. On the other hand, community institutions usually have a heavy task load in communities where there is a high population density and relatively infrequent contact with outsiders, resulting in a high need for cooperation. Ethnographic evidence, for example, shows that among sedentary agricultural groups, such as the Hopi Indians in the southwestern United States, community-wide institutions are especially important in organizing a wide range of social and political activities. The particular pattern of settlement and agricultural production among the Hopi makes a high level of contact and cooperation among individuals important in day-to-day life (Simmons 1963).

4. This does not mean that tribalism was no longer a factor in the Copperbelt towns, however. Epstein (1958) points out that in the competition for union positions the various coalitions formed were almost always tribally based.

Secondly, some communities have institutions which are more effective than those of other communities, although this variable is often difficult to measure. Perceived effectiveness, from the perspective of community members, is probably much more important as a measure of institutional strength than is an objective appraisal of institutional efficiency. Effectiveness refers not only to the perception that institutions are doing what they are supposed to do, but also to the extent to which individuals see them as responsive to their demands and needs. Edelman suggests that an effective leader is one who is active and who gives the impression of attempting to solve the problems confronting him; one who indicates that he cannot cope with problems is bound to be seen as ineffective (1964:chap. 5). The specific results are less important than the appearance of being in control, he contends.

One of the most crucial aspects of the political integration process is that institutional capabilities must rise faster than demands during the early stages. Institutions that are not strong, in the sense of being able to solve problems, are not likely to gain continued support. In learning-theory terms, the ability of institutions to provide positive reinforcement to the members of the community is likely to lead to further support for the institutions and to the strengthening of feelings of community (Deutsch 1957).

Spillover and task expansion

Task expansion by existing organizations can be a crucial aspect of increasing integration. Organizations with aggressive leaders may come to undertake new functions, or to create entirely new organizations. While some early students of integration stressed the almost automatic manner in which task expansion leads to increased integration (Haas 1958; Mitrany 1966), more recent analyses have pointed out a number of ways in which the spillover process is far from automatic (Haas 1964, 1970;

Nye 1970, 1971; Schmitter 1969). The initial position stressed the ways in which integrative lessons learned in one functional context could be transferred to new contexts, where there are individuals who desire to make the connection. Another mechanism of task expansion is that initial functional tasks often contain their own expansive logic (Haas 1964). Success in one domain creates a spillover potential leading to increased integration in other areas.

Neofunctionalists have come to understand the importance of institutions as well as integrative lessons in the spillover process (Nye 1971:51). While emphasizing welfare and technical questions, the neofunctionalist realizes that these have important political implications and that integration increases when these linkages are made. At the same time, Nye and other neofunctionalists criticize federalist integration strategies, which they believe overstress legalistic and constitutional questions of sovereignty, often arousing resistance before the time when new needs have developed (Nye 1971:50). The thrust of the neofunctionalist position is to push for task expansion within existing institutional arrangements while at the same time recognizing that the "logic of task expansion" is not sufficient to bring it about (Lindberg and Scheingold 1970:chap. 1).

Criticism of the earlier position has produced an articulation of conditions inhibiting, as well as promoting, task expansion and spillover, and suggesting reasons why spillover is often far from automatic. Haas (1970:11) suggests that successful accomplishments in many fields of potentially integrative activity can result in "self-encapsulation" organizationally and attitudinally. A second possibility is that the success of one organization leads to the creation of rival organizations. Nye suggests that as integration moves to higher levels, the process should become more political and hence less amenable to technocratic decision-making (1970:218-19). Redefinition of tasks does not necessarily mean an upgrading of interests, as increased transactions can lead to an increase in burdens rather than to spillover (Nye

35

1970:201–6). Thus, decision-makers committed to a set of institutions may not necessarily be able to increase the over-all level of integration through spillover (Schmitter 1970:240–42).

Community and political integration: conceptual parallels

The concepts of community and political integration are quite similar. The level of community in an area is seen as dependent on four elements: (1) its association with a particular geographic area; (2) the identification of that area by its inhabitants as socially or politically distinct; (3) the presence of regular and identifiable social relations and institutions in the area; and (4) the absence of a single goal as the focal point of the territory's organization. The second and third elements in this definition are conceptually parallel to two aspects of Deutsch's defintion of political integration—the development of a sense of community and the presence of institutions and practices strong enough to ensure the peaceful settlement of disputes. The first and fourth elements of the definition of community are absent in discussions of political integration.

Almost all studies of political integration are concerned with the national and international levels. To include in their considerations the problem of whether or not there is an identifiable geographic area associated with the community, or whether or not the community is single-purposed, would not be very worthwhile. At the more local level, however, these elements of the definition become important in permitting a distinction between a small village and, say, a large factory. The factory has well-developed institutions and practices to ensure the peaceful settlement of disputes, a sense of community, and even an identifiable territory. Unlike the village, however, its organization is highly specific in purpose. Thus, the absence of these questions from the integration literature does not mean that the concepts of community and political integration are not highly parallel.

In this study of Mathare 2, the major interest in community is in those elements which are also the concern of the integration theorists—the sense of community and the institutions found there. The other two aspects of community can be considered much more briefly and are not our major interest. The geographical area known as Mathare 2 is clearly identified, although its outer borders are somewhat unclear. On two sides it joins villages 1 and 3, each sharing a kind of no-man's-land not clearly part of either village. The third side runs into the river, which some people see as the limit of the community, while the boundary on the fourth is Juja Road or private property. The general purposes of the over-all social and political organization are described in detail below.

Our immediate concern is the understanding of squatters and squatter settlements as an important form of urban growth in Africa, Asia, and Latin America. Reviewing existing studies, we can begin to understand some of the elements shared by these areas in diverse geographical settings, and to develop an outline of the process of community formation experiences that can guide the investigation of sources of political integration in Mathare 2.

3

Urban squatters in developing nations

The percentage of the world's population living in cities is increasing at an unprecedented rate. Between 1950 and 1960 the proportion of the population living in cities with 100,000 or more inhabitants rose twice as fast as it did in the preceding fifty years (Davis 1968). The fastest rates of urban growth are found in the cities of Africa, Asia, and Latin America, in contrast to Europe and North America where the growth curves of the largest cities have flattened out or even turned downward (Davis 1957).

Population figures indicate important shifts in human distribution, and also serve as an extremely visible indicator of other widespread changes taking place in a society. As urbanization increases, so does the scale of a society, and there are changes in the ways individuals, groups, and communities relate to each other (Wilson and Wilson 1965; Greer 1962; van Hoey 1968). The increasing scale of an urbanizing society means that life styles in rural as well as urban areas are altered. Previously self-sufficient agricultural people become peasant farmers, specializing in a particular crop and selling their products in a market town. When they are drawn into the cash economy, their consumption patterns change, traditional ways of doing things are modified, formal education spreads, and children learn values often very different from those of their parents.

In such a context the city is a magnet. It is the center of change, the setter of fashions, the birthplace of new ideas, and, most important, the place to make money. Generally the reality does not live up to the attraction, however, for there are few cities in which there are more jobs and houses than there are people to fill them. The result is that while the rural image of urban opportunities is often an optimistic one, and while there is a certain percentage of the urban population who "make it big," there is often an even larger number who get stuck in the revolving door of social change and never escape.

Not all social changes in urbanizing societies are intended or desirable. People get caught in social situations they can neither understand nor control. They become dislocated or trapped between two ways of life, and are unable to participate fully in either. These people are drawn into cities for a variety of reasons. Some have literally nowhere else to go. Others are searching for an environment where children will have a greater chance of becoming educated and leading a better life than their parents. Still others come to the city to get a taste of adventure, to explore a bit, to taste life in a new environment; they do not necessarily come with the intention of staying there permanently, but after a few years they "can't leave." Finally, there are individuals who simply grow up in the city, and know no other way of life.

Most migrants to the city leave relatively well-integrated rural communities in which there is a strong sense of community as well as a wide range of community institutions (although the integration of these rural communities does not mean that they could meet all the needs of community members). Typically, urban neighborhoods are places to sleep, rather than integrated political communities, but this is not always the case. In most cities there are zones where social interaction is intense, where residents are highly dependent on one another for social survival, and where there develop a sense of community and a set of local institutions serving a wide range of needs. Often these are found in squatter communities in developing nations, where the combined stress of daily living and threats of intervention from the outside brings people closer together. In seeking to understand this pattern, we move from a discussion of the causes of rapid urban growth in developing nations to an analysis of the formation and development of squatter communities, and finally to a consideration of the forces affecting their internal structure and organization.

Explanations for urban growth

In country after country in Africa, Asia, and Latin America urban growth rates are usually at least double those for the rural areas. Furthermore, it is clear that urban growth is far outdistancing the ability of governments to ensure the provision of housing facilities, services (water supply, garbage collection, sewage, and roads), or jobs. Available evidence indicates that at least a third of the urban work force in developing nations will be unable to move from marginal to steady employment in the next two decades (Nelson 1969:30-34).

Given this setting, why are cities growing so quickly? Why do migrants pour into the urban areas when the chances of their finding steady jobs and adequate housing for their families are so low? Answers to these questions generally take two forms, often referred to as "push" and "pull." The "push" answer suggests that life is so bad in the rural areas that individuals know there is no chance for improvement. Push factors include such conditions as the low productivity of the land or the fact that a man must share his father's land with four or five brothers, so that his own share is a plot too small to be productive. In short, the push factors operate by pushing people out of the rural areas. The "pull" answer emphasizes reasons why the city attracts immigrants, focusing on the prospects for a steady cash income, the existence of better schools for children, or simply the "bright lights" theory, which stresses the excitement of being where the action is. As traditional patterns of social organization weaken, the attractions of the big city are seen as irresistible. Thus, the "pull" factors include the positive attractions of the city, as opposed to the "push" factors, which are the negative aspects of rural life.

The push and pull factors do not operate independently. In fact, it is reasonable to suggest that they may often be mutually reinforcing. When economic opportunities in the rural areas are poor, the prospect of working in the city—even in a menial part-time job—may be relatively attractive. This suggests that both the push and pull factors are related to the specific urbanizing context in each country. Consequently, in explaining the growth of cities in developing nations in recent decades, a number of general contributing factors can be listed, although their relative importance seems to depend upon local conditions.

"Push" factors

People leave the rural areas for the following reasons:

1. It becomes impossible to earn enough for subsistence on their own land. This may be due to diminishing productivity of overfarmed land, division of the land into unproductive units through inheritance, economic reversals, or natural disasters.

2. It becomes impossible to earn enough for subsistence when individuals working as laborers on large farms or plantations are displaced by technological innovations. (In some cases a man or his children may see these changes coming and make the decision to move, realizing what the future will be in the rural areas.)

3. They are deviants in the local social structure. They may be members of a religious or ethnic minority, women who are barren, or men who are branded publicly as thieves or outlaws.

4. They are victims of the social dislocation caused by wars, revolutions, political agitation, or social ferment.

5. They are forced to move by the government or other powerful groups in the society.

In each of these situations, individuals leaving their rural homes will not necessarily become urban migrants. They may move to rural areas in another part of the country, or become migrant farm workers. Alternatively, they may leave the agricultural sector and become small traders or craftsmen in their own or another rural community. The number of urban migrants produced when any of these factors is present, then, varies across situations.

"Pull" factors

People go to the cities for the following reasons:

1. They believe they can earn a cash income that is higher than that available in the rural areas. This seems equally important for people with very high and very low levels of education.

2. They feel that there will be better opportunities for education and employment for their children.

3. They have heard stories of urban life from relatives and friends, and want to experience it themselves.

4. They wish to enjoy the technological features of modern society, which are mainly confined to the urban areas.

Migrants to cities are not generally under the illusion that they or their children will become rich men simply by living in town. They recognize that this happens to only a few. What they do generally contend is that while only a few "make it" in town, almost no one in their position in the rural community will see any change in his life at all.

Migration choices, whether motivated by push or pull factors, are not necessarily irrevocable. In the developing nations, many young men have visited the city several times before making the decision to look for work there. Some will move to the city, then reject city life and return to the rural areas. For others, life in the city may represent a stage in the life cycle. They may live and work in the city to earn enough money to pay for the education of their children or to buy a larger farm; when these goals are accomplished, they will return to the country. Thus urban life should not necessarily be seen as a permanent rejection of traditional values or rural life styles.[1]

Why do they stay?

If the push and pull factors help account for the high levels of migration to cities in developing nations, they do not fully explain why so many migrants remain as marginal participants in the urban society, living in conditions of extreme poverty. Why do so many urban migrants stay? While the importance of specific factors varies from place to place, the most important reasons for their staying in the city are as follows:

1. They have no rural alternatives to turn to. They may have no land rights, or they may own land that is either too unproductive or too small to support them and their families.

2. They lack the skills needed to work in agriculture.

3. They think that conditions in the city will be better—at least for their children—in the future.

4. They like city life.

5. Their standard of living is higher than that which they could maintain in the rural areas, despite the fact that they may

1. It appears that the level of interaction and movement between rural and urban areas is higher in Africa and Asia than in Latin America.

be extremely poor, unemployed, and living at a subsistence level.

6. They are participants in a social system (their neighborhood, or an ethnic or religious community) in which they have established ties and expectations, and which they do not want to leave.

Even when conditions are seen as bad in the city, rural alternatives are perceived as worse (Leeds and Leeds 1970). If people in the city are poor, those in the rural areas are poverty stricken. If urban education and health facilities are inadequate, in the rural areas they are almost nonexistent. Consequently, the number of people leaving cities is far smaller than those entering, despite the fact that a cursory analysis of employment and housing opportunities suggests that migrants are not needed and cannot be taken care of. In fact, in many countries the major brake on further urban growth today may be these well-known conditions, and their improvement could unleash new waves of urban migration.

An analysis of the forces affecting urban growth in any particular situation requires information about who the migrants are, and usually leads to the realization that there is a great deal of diversity within the migrant population, just as there is in the permanent urban population. Some migrants are pushed out of the rural areas because of the poverty of the land, while others may be the offspring of relatively well-to-do peasants who are able to educate their children and who are attracted to the increased opportunities in the city. Thus, the calculus of the relative advantages of city life is hardly the same for all individuals.

Decisions whether or not to migrate result from different antecedent conditions. It cannot be said, then, that migrants are clearly those people least able to subsist in the countryside. In fact, in some situations, just the opposite is the case. The migrant who is relatively unskilled in comparison with longer-term urban dwellers often is better trained and better educated than the majority of people living in the rural community he is leaving. One study found that:

> in India the propensity to migrate to urban areas is much higher among literate and educated people than among the illiterate, and that as the level of education rises the tendency to travel greater distances to employment increases. (Bogue and Zachariah 1962:53)

Thus, to understand the choices that migrants make, more data are needed about their perceptions of the different choices open to them, and the different probabilities associated with these alternatives.[2]

Conditions of urban squatting

The rapid growth of urban areas in developing countries presents severe dilemmas to political decision-makers. The expanding population needs additional social services, housing, and jobs, most of which people supply for themselves in the rural areas (or do without). Most governmental authorities would like to supply these to the migrants to improve their living conditions, for they are aware of the supposed dangers of having large numbers of urban poor who are underfed, unhoused, and unemployed. At the same time, economic advisers point out that large

2. In addition to the push and pull factors, migration rates are partly determined by predispositions to migrate, which are higher in some cultures than in others. Thus, given a particular condition, such as a long drought, individuals from different cultures may respond with differential rates of migration to cities (Segal 1970:66). Variation in the importance of various push and pull factors in determining migration rates is a function of objective economic, social, and political conditions and of particular cultural frameworks through which these conditions are interpreted. Morse quotes Germani as suggesting that objective conditions "are filtered through the attitudes and decisions of individuals. . . . Therefore rural-urban migration is not merely a symptom, a demographic fact and a response to a certain economic pressure, but also the expression of a mental change" (Morse 1966:44).

capital investments in urban communities drain off development funds that would yield a far higher return in other parts of the country. There is a continual conflict between improving social conditions in the large cities and investing money in more economically appealing ways.

In most situations the conflict is never fully resolved. Governments invest some of their resources in expanding urban services and facilities, but not enough to keep up with the demands of the rapidly growing population. To cope with inadequate services, people living in cities have developed a number of indigenous responses. In many urban communities there are associations, both formal and informal, formed by migrants from a common ethnic group or region. These serve as social welfare agencies, assisting members in times of need and tiding them over rough periods. A migrant arriving in town drifts into such an organization gradually. He may first live with a kinsman from his home area, who usually introduces the migrant to his friends in the city and helps him find work. Where there are voluntary associations which have regular meetings, the migrant is introduced to other members, and often he is asked to share some of the news from home with the group. As his stay in the city lengthens, the new migrant becomes a member of the organization, pays his dues regularly, and is eligible for help if he should lose his job or need a loan for sudden expenses (Mangin 1965a; Little 1965; Doughty 1970).

A second characteristic way of coping with the social conditions in the city is through the formation of new communities, which aim to relieve the overcrowding and filth of center-city slum dwellings and to give people a more permanent home. These uncontrolled and initially unregulated communities are located wherever empty land is available—usually, but not always, in the peripheral areas of the city. Such settlements, built by the residents themselves without any government assistance, on land that they neither own nor occupy legally, are found in large cities throughout the world. What these settlements have in common is that their population is usually living in conditions that are better than those found in center-city slums, and that they represent initiative taken by city residents to cope with the overcrowding and inadequate services found in the city.

Sometimes planners view such communities as indications of a certain "phase" of development, as temporary blemishes on the face of the city, rather than as a more permanent or enduring phenomenon. Their policies, then, become phrased in terms of eradication or liquidation of the settlement; its more basic causes are not dealt with. On the other hand, when governmental officials adopt a more realistic view concerning their ability to manage urban growth, they can often take steps to guide and direct, if not control, the development of new settlements.

Planners can be sensitive to where growth is likely to take place, and can make available such facilities as clean water, garbage collection, police protection, schools, and roads. In the middle sixties in Nairobi, for example, plots in a "site-and-service" scheme located at the edge of the city were offered to squatters in a center-city area about to be destroyed. The new community, Kariobangi, had roads, water supplies, and latrines in neatly laid-out plots. Individuals were rented a plot for a fee of thirty shillings per month, on which they constructed their own houses of either traditional or newer, more expensive materials. The government has since established schools, built shops, and provided other public services in the area. Although the city provided the services usually missing in squatter communities, the cost was kept relatively low because the new owners supplied the capital to construct the houses. By 1970, Kariobangi was a thriving neighborhood with a number of small businesses and shops, and many wooden and stone houses had replaced the original ones.

For the most part, however, this type of new community for the urban poor is an exception. Much more common is the squatter community that the government recognizes only long after it is established. In many cases the community and the government come to some sort of an "understanding," with the government agreeing to supply certain social services because of its awareness of the potential political threat of thousands of homeless people in the city. In some parts of the world, such as Latin America, where a large proportion of the urban population lives in squatter settlements, the process of setting governmental policy and the relationships between the community and the government are well established. In other areas, such as Africa, where squatter communities are not as common, both sides are just beginning to recognize the need to relate to each other.

In Latin American cities, squatter settlements are considered an integral part of urban growth. In most large cities, between 20 and 50 per cent of the population lives in such communities. In Venezuela, for example, about one-third of the population of Caracas and one-half of the population of Maracaibo, the two largest cities in the country, live in *barrios*. In 1966 one study identified 254 separate squatter communities in Caracas and 108 in Maracaibo, most of which had between 1,500 and 2,500 inhabitants (Ray 1969:8). Similar figures probably would be found in studies of other major urban centers in Latin America, such as Lima, Buenos Aires, Mexico City, and Rio de Janeiro.

In Asia, squatters are found in almost every large city. Many of them do not even have a temporary shack where they can sleep. One observer estimated that there were about 600,000 people in Calcutta whose only place to sleep is on the streets (Abrams 1964:3). While squatters make up only 15 to 25 percent of the population—not as large a proportion as in Latin America—they number in the hundreds of thousands: in Djakarta, there are 750,000 (25 per cent); in Delhi, 200,000 (13 per cent); in Kuala Lumpur, 100,000 (20 per cent); in Hong Kong, 580,000

(17 per cent); and in Manila, 320,000 (25 per cent) (Dwyer 1964:153).

Urban squatting is well known and extensive in the *bidonvilles* of North African cities, such as Algiers, but is a much more recent and less developed phenomenon in sub-Saharan black Africa. The most dramatic case is that of Kinshasa (formerly Léopoldville), the capital of Zaïre, where the population rose from about 100,000 in 1946 to 345,000 on the eve of independence in 1960 and to about one million by the late 1960s. A large portion of the population growth occurred in the suburban areas of the city as a result of large-scale squatting (Raymaekers 1964).

Formation and development of squatter settlements

Squatter settlements develop in rapidly growing cities where there is a large gap between the popular demand for housing and that supplied by conventional institutions (Turner 1968a:120). They develop on empty land in the city—in swampy lowlands, on the sides of steep hills, or in vacant lots at the edge of the city. There is a good deal of variation in the ways in which squatter settlements begin. Some grow slowly as people drift into the area in twos and threes, while others are built up literally overnight as the result of a large-scale planned invasion.

In Latin America, where new settlements are continually formed, the process usually pits the ingenuity of the would-be squatters against the institutional structures of government. The most common pattern is an organized invasion of the vacant land, a rapid distribution of plots, and the construction of temporary dwellings, all in a short period of time—often overnight or during a weekend. Once the settlement is started the squatters battle attempts to oust them from the site, either by returning repeatedly after police eviction or by bringing to bear whatever political connections they have.

In Venezuela, according to Ray (1969:33-43), the leaders of the invasion usually have done a careful job of planning. He contends that most successful invasion leaders have secured the backing, at least tacitly, of the political parties in power in the city—a step aimed at protecting the community and its leader from official reprisal. In situations where different political coalitions are in power at the provincial and municipal levels in Venezuela, the squatters manage to play one group against the other to obtain support for their moves (Ray 1969:34-35). Invasion leaders are usually well aware of the status of the land they seize, and will take steps to make their partisan links more explicit when they feel their security of tenure may be weak. Ray describes an invasion of a large plot of land outside Maracaibo just after the 1964 elections in Venezuela; the invasion leaders posted large signs announcing the formation of "Barrio Raul Leoni," named after the newly inaugurated president (1969:37).

There are two systems of land distribution in new settlements in Venezuela. In areas where the site is relatively large and flat, newcomers to the community generally seek out the invasion leaders, who distribute land marked out in neat squares (about thirty by sixty feet) with at least one side on a street. When the site is hilly, the leaders generally lay out only a rough street pattern in the area, and allow new settlers to crowd in as well as they can, with the size of plots being inversely related to the total demand (Ray 1969:38). The significance of the difference is that in settlements where the flat terrain permits the leaders to supervise tightly the allocation of plots, they establish their authority at an early stage. In hilly areas, where the invasion leaders exercise far less control over the distribution of land, they are much less likely to be able to establish authority in the community.

The invasion and settlement process is sometimes highly complicated. Turner describes one invasion in Lima, Peru, where the police chased several hundred invaders off the land but allowed them to camp temporarily along a nearby railway embankment while the leaders negotiated with the authorities. Five weeks later, on Christmas Eve, the squatters were permitted to set up a temporary encampment on part of the land. At the same time the leaders hired five topographers at a cost of $1,000 to lay out plots for houses. Once the layout was completed the families moved to the plots they were allocated (1970:6). Further improvements in the community followed quickly thereafter:

> As soon as the encampment on the site was established, the association organized a school which provided primary education to adults as well as to children, and many set up shops for vermicelli, candles, inca-coal, and other essentials. At first everything, including water, had to be carried up a footpath, but once the families had moved to their own plots an access road was made through the cultivated land which separated the site from the main road in spite of the landowners' protests. (Turner 1970:7)

A less common pattern in Latin America, often found in other parts of the world where there are fewer squatter settlements, is one where a few families or homeless individuals drift into a site and settle. This is most likely to take place in cities where governmental authorities present no active opposition to the squatters, who in turn lack the organizational basis to resist efforts to oust them from the land (Mangin 1967:69).

In Léopoldville (Congo), where in the period immediately after independence the number of squatters rose dramatically, the pattern of settlement is quite different from the typical Latin American one. Local chiefs in the peripheral areas of the city, realizing that sooner or later their land was going to become public property, decided to divide it into lots and sell them to people from the central city who were looking for land to settle on. The sale and occupation of the land did not have the government approval necessary for it to be considered legal. Therefore, most squatters found themselves to be living on land which they had actually purchased but which was not considered theirs by the administration. Having purchased the land, the squatter would regularly come out from the center city to clear it and build a dwelling. During this period he would usually bring his wife and children to help, and he began to develop ties with his neighbors who were engaged in similar tasks. Often the hard work reinforced feelings of interdependence, which already existed among members of a given ethnic group. Sometimes, since some areas developed out of traditional villages on the periphery of the city, there was a tribal chief already in the area, which also helped to create bonds of community among the squatters. Thus the squatter already felt a sense of community by the time the building was completed and he could leave his rented unit in the city to move his family into the new home (Raymaekers 1964).

Government reaction to the formation of a squatter settlement can range from acceptance of the community and an effort to provide social services to its inhabitants to the eviction of the squatters and destruction of their temporary homes. Because of the illegal status of most squatter communities at the outset, leaders are aware of this wide range of possible governmental responses. In many cases, the public governmental position may be to oppose the squatters, while the leaders of the community are developing working relationships with governmental officials behind the scenes. Just because a government has chosen not to destroy a settlement in one part of the city, however, does not necessarily mean that it will take this position in all other areas. In Nairobi, for example, the government has repeatedly burned down squatters' temporary dwellings in Kamakunji, near the center of the city, and at the same time permitted squatters to settle in Mathare Valley and Langata. In Venezuela, Ray reports that squatters usually understand the differential reaction that the government is likely to have toward settlements on public land, privately owned Venezuelan land, and foreign-owned land (1969:36-37). In summary, the government's reaction to the initial formation of a squatter settlement is partially a function of the political connections the settlement's leaders have with the authorities, the size of the invasion force and the political muscle it represents, and the specific site the squatters select.

Developmental patterns

Just as there is wide variation in the initial settlement process, there are also marked differences in the development of squatter communities. Turner (1968a) distinguishes between provisional communities and incipient, self-improving communities on the basis of the degree of permanence of building materials and the availability of public services. While all communities begin as provisional settlements, Turner suggests that the developmental pattern is a function of the location of the community within the urban area, and of the characteristics of its population (1968a; 1968c).

Within any urban area, settlements in the more peripheral regions are most likely to become self-improving, incipient communities. The land on which they are located is usually of relatively low value, and thus population densities are likely to be fairly low and the community more or less free from governmental harassment in making plans for improvements. Communities which fail to develop beyond the provisional stage are most likely to be located near employment centers of the unskilled or semiskilled in a variety of physical settings in the city: near central business districts, on marginal lands (hillsides, marshes, unguarded and unused plots of private land), or in marginal neighborhoods near industrial areas. Usually the land is of relatively high value because of its nearness to sources of employment. Noting the great differences between these two types of squatter areas, Turner says:

There are millions of shacks that are neither built nor occupied by squatters and there are hundreds and thousands of squatters who do not live in shacks but solidly built houses. The squatter shantytowns—the really dense and slummy kind referred to as "provisional squatter settlements"—often have far more in common with the traditional downtown slumlord tenements than with the self-improving squatter settlement which is transforming itself into a soundly built neighborhood. And the latter—"self-improving" settlements—often have far more in common with orthodox residential suburbs than they do with shantytowns. (1968a:107)

There are likely to be important differences in the resources, motivations, and backgrounds of the people living in provisional and incipient squatter communities.[3] Provisional settlements, where housing is impermanent and public services are minimal, generally serve the poorest settlers, often those who are either unemployed or underemployed. Center-city provisional settlements are slums in which there is often low social solidarity, where residents see their stay as temporary and seek escape (Portes 1971:239). In contrast, in improving settlements, particularly those in the more peripheral areas, residents often develop a strong psychological commitment to the community (Portes 1971:240), they usually have higher resources for improvement, and they are particularly interested in establishing security of land tenure. In this way they can:

invest their savings and protect themselves from some of the consequences of unemployment—eviction and homelessness, which can have far more serious social and psychological consequences for the established and self-respecting household than for the very poor who have nothing to lose and no status to defend. (Turner 1968a:117)

3. These differences should be observable even after controlling for the age of the community, and are not particularly interesting when comparing communities of different ages. A meaningful comparison might involve a seven-year-old provisional community, located near the center of a city, and an incipient community of the same age in a more peripheral area.

Residence in an uncontrolled settlement has different meaning to inhabitants, depending on their economic conditions. Turner suggests three types of residents with different demands and needs, characteristically found in different proportions in provisional and incipient settlements. *Bridgeheaders* are the economically unestablished, whose most immediate problem is subsistence; they are most often found in central-city provisional settlements near industrial areas where work can be found, near markets where residents can engage in petty commerce, in areas where such services as prostitution or the supplying of illegal alcoholic beverages are in great demand, or even near empty land where subsistence agriculture is possible. *Consolidators* are those with a status to defend, who seek permanent ownership and residence (1968a:117). *Status-seekers* have relatively high incomes and permanent employment, and are seeking a modern standard of amenity in their housing (1968b:358).

As a settlement moves from provisional to incipient status, important changes are likely to appear in the make-up of the population, the physical structure of the community, and the relationship between the community and the wider society (Mangin 1967; Turner 1968c). Early residents are likely to be provincially born adults who have spent several years in the central-city areas before becoming squatters. In the early months the residents are all owner-occupiers and all units are dwellings predominantly populated by nuclear families. There is a feeling of separateness from the city, a feeling of being under attack, as municipal services and protection are lacking and public attitudes are unfavorable. One consequence is that there is likely to be a high degree of community integration, pride in the considerable achievements of the community, and satisfaction with home ownership. Community organizations are headed by the original invasion leaders and are based mainly on the personality of the members plus kinship and regional loyalty (Mangin 1965b:549).

As the community develops, a greater proportion of the popu-

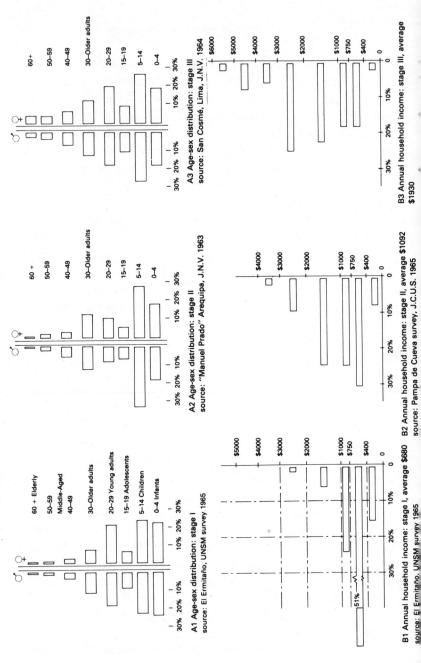

FIGURE 3.1 DEVELOPMENTAL PATTERNS OF SQUATTER SETTLEMENTS

A1 Age-sex distribution: stage I
source: El Ermitaño, UNSM survey 1965

A2 Age-sex distribution: stage II
source: "Manuel Prado" Arequipa, J.N.V. 1963

A3 Age-sex distribution: stage III
source: San Cosmé, Lima, J.N.V. 1964

B1 Annual household income: stage I, average $680
source: El Ermitaño, UNSM survey 1965

B2 Annual household income: stage II, average $1092
source: Pampa de Cueva survey, J.C.U.S. 1965

B3 Annual household income: stage III, average $1930

56

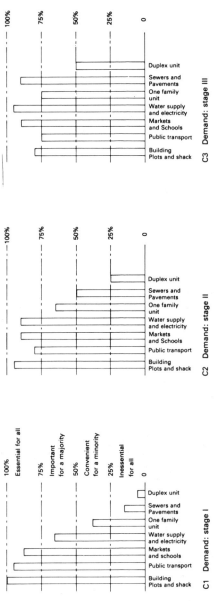

C1 Demand: stage I

100% — Essential for all
75% — Important for a majority
50% — Convenient for a minority
25% — Inessential for all
0

Duplex unit
Sewers and Pavements
One family unit
Water supply and electricity
Markets and schools
Public transport
Building Plots and shack

C2 Demand: stage II

Duplex unit
Sewers and Pavements
One family unit
Water supply and electricity
Markets and Schools
Public transport
Building Plots and shack

C3 Demand: stage III

Duplex unit
Sewers and Pavements
One family unit
Water supply and electricity
Markets and Schools
Public transport
Building Plots and shack

The essential lesson that I learned through long association with barriada-builders was how to distinguish between the architecture of moulds and the architecture of systems. Because the architecture of the barriada is based on a system it can respond to changing demands and it places itself in the hands of the user—it is a vehicle that he can drive in many alternative and unforeseeable directions. This cannot be said for the superficially sophisticated project which governments sponsor with the vain intent of eradicating barriadas.

Charts A1, A2, and A3 show one aspect of the social change that takes place: the barriada is established by young families with a high proportion of very young children; after passing through an intermediate stage when the ratio of infants has dropped and the average age of the adults has risen, the local population structure is similar to that of the city as a whole. After 10 or 15 years, the barriada population is spread across the generations and is balanced between the sexes in the pattern typical of cities in rapidly urbanizing countries. These demographic changes, together with the changes of household structure, translate into changing demands for schools, health services, transportation, and so on, as well as for the volume and organization of domestic living space.

Charts B1, B2, and B3 show the changes of income and income distribution that commonly occurs during the barriada development period. Very young families who establish the barriada have low or very low incomes; they are upwardly mobile,

57

however, and their incomes increase substantially over time—if the three different cases of the same type of settlement (at three stages of development) are as representative as I believe, the average household income trebles during the most rapid development period. As the majority of the permanently resident families enjoy rising incomes, the socio-economic spread or heterogeneity of the population increases, along with the density, intensity and diversity of activities.

Charts C1, C2, and C3 show the changing demand and, by inference, the changing priorities for the basic components of the physical environment. Each column on the charts represents the percentage of the population, at each stage, that both demands and has the material means to obtain or to use the component. A study of the incomes and family structure of the incipient *barriada* in the context of Lima (which, for instance, has a very mild climate and virtually no rainfall) soon leads to the conclusion that the highest priorities are for building land, transportation, and local community facilities—all of which are cheap and all of which are essential for the low-income family moving from an inner-city, rented slum to a peripheral *barriada*. With these components, the family can live, and generally much better than in the worst kind of slum, erecting a provisional shack and buying water delivered by lorry. A decade later, however, the vast majority can afford the full complement of modern utilities; the increased density also makes their installation necessary, just as increased income levels and status heighten the demand. It takes the average family at least 10 years to complete the ground-floor, first stage of their house and it is only when the structure is well advanced that the full complement of installations is required. The demand for rental accommodation grows, at the expense of owner-occupier properties, as the area diversifies and as land values increase. Opportunities for local employment will also increase, especially for those with very low incomes who cannot afford to build or own a property at the level achieved and who, therefore, demand rental accommodation. This demand is met by original settlers seeking secondary sources of income who sub-divide and sub-let their property in part. Although this process often results in slums that really are a health menace, there is no intrinsic reason why this should be so; sensibly regulated, it provides an economic and socially viable answer to an acute problem.

D Schedule of barriada development at the three selected points in time (or stages)

Stage I: at 1–2 years (incipient)	Stage II: at 4–5 years (developing)	Stage III: at 10–12 years (completing)
Land surface		
20–30 ft × 60–80 ft *plots* allotted to each participant family on condition that it is permanently occupied by them	No change	Some *subdivision of plots* in response to growing demand for rental accommodation and individual needs for capital and/or reduced space requirements as families shrink
Sites designated for anticipated community facilities; *public squares* serve as playfields, etc.		
Streets 30–60 ft wide with rectangular grid varying between 150–250 × 250–300 ft		

MARC HOWARD ROSS

THE POLITICAL INTEGRATION OF URBAN SQUATTERS

The booming urban centers in the developing nations of Africa, Asia, and Latin America represent both the promise and the frustration of rapid social change. In response to unprecedented conditions of urban growth, squatter communities have sprung up to provide housing for millions. Mathare Valley Village 2 is a squatter settlement in Nairobi, Kenya, which exemplifies the new social forms and institutions now being created to serve human needs for a population without viable rural alternatives or the prospect of urban security.

Drawing on national and international theories of political integration, Professor Ross outlines the process by which this community, led by former Mau Mau freedom fighters, developed into a politically integrated community where most observers would expect to find disorganization. The residents of Mathare Valley Village 2 have a marginal existence constantly threatened from the outside, as the major economic activity is the brewing and sale of the illegal beer (*pombe*). The in-depth analysis of this squatter community serves to evaluate the generality of theoretical concepts of community formation at the local level.

Marc Howard Ross is Assistant Professor of Political Science at Bryn Mawr College.

ISBN 0—8101—0409—1 $8.50

African Urban Studies

Communications	Regular *omnibus services* are provided as soon as the land is occupied if, as is usual, the site is adjacent to an existing route; *communal taxis* (*colectivos*) often owned by residents provide additional service	No change	No change in transportation services (except for frequency with changing intensity of demand) *Telephones* for public use are generally installed at this stage and, if the area is large enough, a *post office*
Community facilities	A local market and many small *stores and bars* are established at the time of occupation; *primary schools* are also organized and put into immediate operation (with volunteer or locally contracted teachers if necessary); a *chapel* or *shrine* is set up and neighbouring priests are invited to officiate	Commercial facilities are expanded and complemented by *artisan workshops* for domestic and building trades; TV sets with private generators provide local *cinema* services; a *parish centre* is often instituted providing many additional services: additional schooling, health, etc., as well as religious; locally instituted primary schools are adopted by the State and *additional schools* are provided; *medical treatment* will be provided by visiting doctors and dentists and a local *pharmacy* will be established	More specialized commercial facilities are established if the population is large enough—e.g., *commercial banks, specialized stores, cinemas, restaurants*, etc. Local workshops will develop into *small industries*, e.g., for the manufacture of furniture, delivery tricycles, etc. Day *nurseries* are often set up with outside agency help and *clinics* fully installed; all professional services will be available locally
Structures	Initially all structures are *provisional* but starts on permanent dwelling structures are made at the earliest possible moment in order to consolidate claims and invest savings before purchasing power diminishes	During the first years the *shell of a first floor* is generally completed enclosing an average of 1100 sq. ft. of roofed space; permanent *school structures* are built during the first years	After about 10 years the ground floor *one-family unit is completed* and a (potentially independent) *second floor is started*; commercial and public buildings will be completed or built to modern standards
Public utilities	Initially *water* for domestic and construction use must be brought by lorry and sold by the 50-gallon drum (at about 1 s. per drum); no other "utility" is provided at this stage	Considerable and occasionally successful efforts are made at a relatively early stage to obtain *water mains* and *mains electricity*; more frequently water continues to be brought by lorry but local electric generators are set up to supply immediate neighbours	*Water mains, mains electricity, sewers*, and the *surfacing of main roads* may be completed during this period

The schedule of actual development (Chart D) is self-explanatory and confirms the environmental "fit" or "response" of the progressively developing *barriada*. It is not a perfect fit, of course, either socially or economically and however enthusiastic one may be over the qualities emphasized in this article, the architectural form of the planned *barriadas* leaves much to be desired.

SOURCE: This figure has been taken from John C. Turner, "The Squatter Settlement: Architecture That Works," *Architectural Design*, XXXVIII, no. 8 (August, 1968), 358, and is used with the permission of the author and *Architectural Design*.

lation comes directly from rural areas, often on the advice and with the assistance of relatives already living in the settlement. Renting becomes more frequent; families take in relatives and boarders. Stores and bars are opened in homes, and public buildings are constructed. The feeling of separateness lessens as services increase, and belongingness diminishes as the need for unity against the outside threat subsides. Community organizations become more political, their ties with national politics increase, and their over-all strength declines (Mangin 1962:549-50).

Turner suggests three stages of development (incipient, one to two years; developing, four to five years; and completing, ten to twelve years) associated with changes in land surface, communications, community facilities, structures, and public utilities, as well as differences in age and sex distribution, household income, and demands for public services (Figure 3.1). The stages parallel the functions the communities serve, with the incipient stage serving the needs of the bridgeheader, the developing stage serving the consolidator, and the completing stage serving the status-seeker, as the community becomes more an urban neighborhood, integrated into the structure of the larger urban area (Turner 1968c:358).[4]

An external force affecting the developmental pattern of a

4. Turner compares three communities of different ages at the same point in time, in an attempt to get an insight into the longitudinal developmental pattern. Whether the development of a single community follows this pattern is still an empirical question. A related question concerning the generalizability of Turner's model is the extent to which Lima's experience is typical of other cities in developing nations. Nelson (personal communication) suggests that Turner's "theory about migrants' settling first in the center of the city or where they have access to casual jobs, and only later moving to fringe squatter settlements, has been repeated without verification for other Latin cities."
Perlman interviewed residents in three communities in Rio de Janeiro and found little support for the proposition that migrants move from bridgehead to consolidation settlements after they have been in the city for a long time. Instead, she finds a "relative absence of post-migration mobility" within the city, as only one-fifth of her sample had moved more than once within the city after their arrival (1971:27).

settlement is the role of the government. The government can provide the community with services which members are unable to organize or pay for themselves, services which help move the community from the status of a provisional to an incipient settlement. Most common among appeals for governmental assistance are requests for the installation of a water supply, for help in building permanent roads and latrines, and for the establishment of schools and clinics.

In Venezuela, one of the first things that the leaders of the community councils do after their election is to present a series of demands for services to the government. Ray (1969) reports that in most cases the government is extremely slow in handling appeals for aid, and the settlement's leaders, who may once have had widespread support, are often discredited for their inability to deliver what they promised. Nonetheless, governmental assistance remains important to long-term community development, because it is only with some of the government-provided services that a community will grow into an area of improvement and consolidation.

Conclusions

The rapid rate of urban growth in Africa, Asia, and Latin America has added to the great pressures upon the already overburdened governments for urban housing and social services. Migration to the cities, as well as high birth rates, has made it virtually impossible for government programs to keep up with popular demands, even in situations where public officials are so inclined. Responding to these realities, urban dwellers have often taken the initiative in providing mutual assistance and in actually constructing their own housing in the city, most often in the form of the illegal squatter settlement.

These communities are probably the dominant form of urban growth in Latin America today, and are increasingly important in Asia and Africa as well. The formation and initial settlement of a community by squatters is a highly political act, often well planned and organized in advance. At the same time, it is necessary to realize that there can be a good deal of variation in the developmental pattern of squatter communities as a function of their location in the urban area, and of the motivations and needs of their residents.

Virtually all settlements are highly provisional at the outset in the sense that houses are built from temporary, makeshift materials, and there are virtually no social services, such as water, education, waste disposal, or health services, available to residents within the community. From his direct observations, mainly in Lima, Turner suggests that communities in high-density center-city areas, often located on land of relatively high value, are least likely to improve greatly beyond this stage, as the security of land tenure is continually threatened and most of the residents are bridgeheaders seeking to gain an economic toehold in the city. In contrast, settlements located in the more outlying areas on less valuable land are likely to attract squatters who are slightly better off economically and more interested in security of land tenure and consolidation. Thus, some settlements move from provisional to incipient community status within a few years as the government comes to grant legal status and land titles to the community, social services become available, and there is an over-all upgrading of dwellings. Similarly, there are marked changes in the age structure, incomes, and, probably most important, the demands and concerns of residents.

The internal structure of squatter communities varies as widely as the physical conditions. Some are integrated political communities in that there is a relatively strong sense of community and a set of political institutions which are significant in the lives of residents. In terms of our theoretical questions concerning the social and political aspects of community formation, we now need to consider the internal structure of squatter communities, and possible explanations for the wide variation.

4

Community organization and political integration in squatter settlements

There is a wide range of myths concerning the politics of squatters, just as there are rumors and stories concerning any separate social group. On the one hand, there are the myths which view squatters, and often the urban poor generally, as disorganized and incapable of meaningful self-help or organization. On the other hand, there is a parallel set of myths which picture the squatters as the cadre of revolutionary leftist political movements (Nelson 1969). While each of these myths, as well as a number of others, can certainly be understood in terms of the needs of dominant groups in any society, there is little to support their validity. In reality, urban squatters are usually more organized than the disorganization hypothesis contends, but often far less organized than the radicalization hypothesis implies.

Organization among squatters is most often concerned with the mundane, day-to-day concerns of community life. Typically in Latin American cities there is a committee of leaders, appointed at the time of invasion, which serves as the provisional government and whose main job is to try to secure legal status and social services from both the city and the central government. In many cases the days immediately following the invasion represent an organizational high point for the community. Factional disputes, rivalries between leaders, and the slowness of government response all serve to weaken the organization. This process of community formation can be analyzed in terms of the two elements of political integration discussed in chapter 2: sense of community and the development of community institutions. By considering the internal structure of squatter communities, as well as important outside influences, forces determining the level of integration can be identified. Although few existing studies undertook this identification, the data they provide can be reinterpreted in developing hypotheses to organize the detailed analysis of Mathare 2. What affects the sense of community and strength of political institutions among squatters?

The squatters

The political integration of squatter communities is partially a function of the distinctiveness of the squatter population. The strength of squatter integration might be expected to be a function of the degree to which they differ from the wider population of the city. Similarly, their backgrounds, motivations, and aspirations may lead them to be relatively aggressive or passive in efforts to achieve community integration. Where most squatters are recent arrivals from the countryside, we might expect political integration to be relatively weak in contrast to a community made up mainly of people with considerable urban experience. To what extent are squatter populations sufficiently homogeneous so that we can make meaningful generalizations about them? What are the significant ways in which squatter populations vary? How reasonable are most common stereotypes about urban squatters?

Migration experience

One of the most widespread beliefs is that squatters are recent migrants to the city. Available data show that this is inaccurate, for while most squatters are migrants they typically have considerable urban experience, usually having lived in center-city slum areas before moving into a squatter settlement. Mangin reports that in a typical *barriada* in Lima, the average length of residence in the city for family heads was nine years, and almost no one had been in Lima for less than three years (Mangin 1967:68; Portes 1971:241). Other studies have reported the same pattern in other Latin American cities—Mexico City, Santo Domingo, Guatemala City, Caracas, Bogotá, Panama City, and Santiago (Mangin 1967:68). For Asia there is a great deal less information, but McGee's (1967) small survey in a settlement in Kuala Lumpur shows the same pattern. All the household heads in his sample were born in rural areas and had originally migrated to other areas of the city; most moved into the squatter settlement when they felt the pressure for greater space—usually after they were married and began to have children.

Homer suggests two complementary explanations for this pattern. First, the highest migration levels are found in the 20-29 age group for men and the 15-24 age group for women. She says that expectations and needs should rise for the migrants as they gain urban experience and enter a stage of the life cycle during which they become responsible for a young and growing family, and that these needs probably peak between five and nine years after migration. The combined pressures of the expectations and needs "might be the impetus required to encourage participation in a squatter invasion" (1971:20). The rewards for success are great, as the squatter will come to acquire his own house and at the same time relieve himself of the regular rent payments he is now making. "The long-term rewards are promising enough to risk considerable hardship, sometimes physical harm, in the short run" (1971:21).

A second factor is that in five to ten years of living in the city the migrant has begun to participate in a wide range of urban social networks. He knows his way around. He is likely to be in contact with others who are equally dissatisfied with

65

their living conditions, and he has probably begun to learn some of the ways in which others have coped with situations similar to his.

> In view of the amount of organization that is involved in these invasions it seems highly unlikely that it is the newly arrived migrant with only the clothes on his back who participates in the establishment of a squatter settlement; rather it seems plausible that his forerunner, experienced in the ways of the city, with access to information channels of an informal type, and with sufficient motivations, will be the man most likely to become a squatter. (Homer 1971:21)

Employment

A second popular belief is that squatters are either unemployed, underemployed, or working in the most menial jobs.[1] While in general this is true, there is a great deal of variation in the pattern. In most countries, urban unemployment is concentrated among the unskilled, and most squatters tend to fall in this category. In Venezuela unemployment rates among adult males in squatter settlements ranged from 15 or 20 per cent to around 75 per cent (Ray 1969:17). In Léopoldville (Kinshasa) unemployment among squatters was between 64 and 73 per cent (Raymaekers 1964:188).[2] In Kuala Lumpur, on the other hand, McGee (1967) reported no unemployment in his small sample, although the squatters held low-status occupations requiring limited skills. Employment figures must be interpreted cautiously, however, for they often include only individuals drawing a regu-

---

1. In Turner's scheme this should be more true for provisional than for incipient communities.
2. Good data on employment in squatter communities are particularly hard to find. In addition, there is a great deal of seasonal variation within a community, as well as variation between communities in the same city. For example, in one community in Kinshasa, Knoop reports that unemployment is approximately 35 per cent, in contrast to the figure Raymaekers offers (1966:143).

lar wage, thus masking both underemployment (Guha 1958:23), on the one hand, and many diverse sources of income which add up to subsistence, on the other.

Some squatters are also landlords, deriving an income from renting either rooms in their own houses or other houses that they own.[3] A second source of income is small-scale services performed within the community. In the squatter settlements in Léopoldville, unemployed squatters performed a number of odd jobs—selling building materials in the squatting areas, chopping wood, repairing bicycles, carrying water, selling drinks, running small shops, and even working as servants for other squatters (Raymaekers 1964:196). In most settlements there is periodic work for individuals with building skills, such as carpenters or roof builders. A small shop selling a variety of consumer goods is often a squatter's major means of support. While the shop may be poorly stocked and the profit margin low, it could provide an income comparable with the wages he would earn as a manual laborer and higher than what he would make as a rural peasant.

Social disorganization

A third image of squatter settlements is that they are centers of illegal activity, organized crime, and social disorganization. The evidence, however, indicates that this is widely exaggerated. Mangin suggests that while petty theft and tax evasion are frequently practiced, organized crime is rare. One reason he offers is that there are often more lucrative areas where criminals can work. There are communities, however, such as Rooiyard (South Africa), where an illegal enterprise such as beer brewing provides a major source of income for the community (Hellmann 1969).

The presence of illegal activities, if they do not represent

3. Most residents in squatter communities in Latin America are owner-occupiers. Mangin (1967:75) reports that over 95 per cent own their own dwellings in Peru, Venezuela, and Brazil.

crimes against persons in general or against settlement residents in particular, is not incompatible with the existence of strong social institutions, both formal and informal, which counters the argument that squatter settlements are zones of social disorganization. Whyte (1966) and Suttles (1968) show the strength of social institutions in poor areas of the city, although the main purposes of some organizations in the community are activities which the wider society considers illegal or unacceptable.

The most important social institutions in squatter settlements are the family and household (usually the same unit), which provide "a degree of crisis insurance" to residents (Mangin 1967: 72). Pearse describes the relationship as one of mutual aid, where each member is "expected to contribute to the common good or 'family wealth' according to his competence" (1961:197). The unemployed are taken care of by relatives (Ray 1969:18), while neighborliness and extrafamilial obligations and ties are avoided in some settlements (Pearse 1961:200). Furthermore, in certain cities the family maintains important links to rural kinsmen through visits and by sending money on a regular basis (McGee 1967:164). These ties permit the squatter to return home or to send his wife and children home if he suffers serious economic or social reversals in the city, although the ties are not usually maintained for this reason alone.

The social characteristics of squatters are partially a function of the type of community in which they live. In Turner's scheme, one would expect a large number of unemployed and underemployed squatters in provisional communities, and a greater percentage of regular wage earners in incipient ones. Similarly, Mangin's hypotheses presented above suggest that new communities are likely to have a higher proportion of provincially born adults with extensive urban experience, whereas in older communities adults are more likely to come directly from the rural areas to stay with a relative upon their arrival in the city. Individuals with different social backgrounds, then, are likely to be the participants in an original squatter invasion than are likely to move into an established community.[4]

Community organization

Community-wide political and social organizations are created in almost every squatter community for which evidence is available, but their activity, public support, and effectiveness vary widely. In many settlements the cooperative activity during the initial invasion and the building of temporary dwellings constitute the high point of local organizational effectiveness. In a smaller number of cases, the initial organizations are sufficiently flexible to continue to serve community needs (Mangin 1967: 70).

The most important jobs for the community political organization are to help secure and defend the land on which the squatters live and to try to secure physical improvements in the area. Initially there is a high level of public support for the leaders as they ask the government for help in the installation of a water supply, for road improvements, and for a school and electricity. Often the response is discouraging. In Venezuela, for example, the government usually does nothing at all for the first year, and then it often provides electricity and street repair before making water available, although the residents consider water to be their most urgent need (Ray 1969:46). The long wait for a response often turns the residents against the committee of leaders.

> Unless the junta is smart or lucky enough to divert the community's attention from obtaining water to another feasible project, thus justifying its continued existence, it eventually ceases its efforts and fades into retirement or disbands completely. Subse-

4. Homer (1971:27) suggests that there may be strong personality differences between the early migrants and the people drawn into an already established squatter community.

quently, when the prospects for success are better, a new group is formed or the old reemerges. (Ray 1969:45)

Local organizational success in getting the government to provide public services and to recognize the tenure rights of the settlers is also likely to have the curious effect of weakening the organization itself. A good deal of the organizational strength and effectiveness in most communities is due to the settlers' insecurity of tenure, and this threat diminishes as the government begins to provide services and security (Turner 1968a:120; Mangin 1967:70). Thus local political organization is stimulated by outside threat. Inability to cope with the problems of public services and security of tenure is likely to lead to local rejection of the organization and to its dissolution. On the other hand, success in coping with the threat is likely to lead to a weakening of the organization as the community becomes integrated into the larger urban system.

Moderate levels of governmental threat to the settlement or slowness in providing services can stimulate greater levels of cooperative activity among the residents (Ray 1969:46). While this may be important in situations where the residents have the skills or materials needed to help themselves, they are often faced with problems they cannot solve locally. At a certain level, threat or harassment is no longer functional to the community. Goldrich et al. discuss one settlement in Lima, "El Espiritu," where a series of pitched battles between police and squatters involved loss of life and property. Armed troops surrounded the community for an additional period, "so that the squatters were under constant fear that attacks would be launched to drive them off the land" (Goldrich, Pratt, and Schuller 1967: 11–12). Subsequent political activity was significantly *lower* in this community than in comparable settlements where such armed confrontations did not take place, which suggests that despite the short-term success of the "El Espiritu" settlers, the levels of threat and traumatization combined to produce depoliticization and withdrawal from politics.

In cases of very low threat or hostility, local organization may fail to develop at all. In a comparison of settlements in Lima and San Juan, Rogler attributed the absence of strong community organization in the Puerto Rican city to the benevolent setting, in comparison with the hostility and adversity faced by the squatters in Peru (cited in Morse 1966:55). Similarly, in Léopoldville no political organizations were found in many of the squatting areas. The only ties that existed were ethnic links and traditions maintained by the squatters themselves (Raymaekers 1964:197). Relations between squatters were often warm and cooperative, in contrast to many Latin American communities where there are strong desires for personal privacy and a disinclination to be involved with individuals outside the family (Ray 1969:chap. 5). Thus, the effect of outside threat or hostility on local organization is probably curvilinear, reaching its peak at moderate levels of threat where it can stimulate political organizations among squatters and help develop a sense of community identification.

Squatters often are successful in achieving their major political goals which are local: the establishment of a community, the obtaining of governmental recognition, and the provision of social services. Despite these successes, they are often apathetic about or uninvolved in politics, and the high level of political efficacy which is manifest in creating their community is rarely seen again (Ray 1969:chap. 5; Mangin 1967; Turner 1968a; Goldrich et al. 1967; Powell 1969).

Because of the marginal nature of squatting, it is commonly assumed that squatters are ready to join extremist political movements which threaten to destroy the existing social order. The evidence, however, is that political involvement is neither higher nor lower than local participation in nonsquatter groups (Nelson 1969; Cornelius 1971). Analysis of voting patterns indicates widespread support for conservative parties and candidates (Mangin 1967:82-85) and suggests that involvement is generally through the machinery of traditional political parties (Morse 1966:57). In Venezuela, after a settlement has achieved initial recognition, much of the local political activity is linked to nonradical national political organizations. In the early 1960s the *Accion Democratica*, one of the ruling parties, was very weak in the cities in general and in the barrios in particular. To strengthen itself the party used patronage, selective attention, and favors in an attempt to control local committees, increase party membership, and strengthen itself before the next elections (Ray 1969:110-27).

Turner explains the lack of political radicalism among squatters by suggesting that bridgeheaders are too preoccupied with their overwhelming personal problems to become involved, while consolidators develop a vested interest in the community (1968a: 119). Sewell, observing squatter organization in Turkey, noted a similar pattern. Government officials and intellectuals frequently suggest that the residents of the *gecekondu* (squatter settlements) will become radicals, but this has not taken place.

> The migrants are principally villagers with a deep devotion to their religion and a surprisingly powerful sense of Turkish nationalism. . . . Secondly, the vast majority of the *gecekondu* residents have accomplished significant social and economic mobility in a relatively short period of time. . . . Thirdly, these migrants have developed a strong sense of responsibility towards their sizeable investment in the *gecekondu,* and they seem anxious to avoid any action or suggestion that would jeopardize themselves, their houses or their community. (Sewell, cited in Turner 1968a:119)

The community in which the squatter lives, then, is not a base from which he hopes to change the world. Instead, it is a means through which he participates in the world more fully. His outlook is still in many ways that of the peasant whose conception of the limited good leads him to be suspicious of nonkinsmen, to maximize his short-term economic interest, and, most of all, to protect his own property. He does what he thinks is necessary to survive, not what he thinks is good for others.

Political integration

Squatter settlements, like other communities, are politically integrated to the extent that their residents develop a sense of community and a set of political institutions capable of handling local problems in a peaceful manner. Their integration can be evaluated in two ways. It is possible to examine the extent of integration into the wider society; some communities may be separated from the rest of the urban area and may be objects of hostility and scorn from the authorities, while others may be more like suburban residential neighborhoods, with residents employed throughout the city and well integrated into its social and political life. Alternatively, we may examine the level of integration *within* the squatter settlement, which is a function of factors affecting the levels of identification with the community and of institutional strength. Our interest is mainly in the second type of integration—that which is internal to the community.

Relatively few studies have explicitly considered the question of internal integration among urban squatter communities, and therefore this discussion will attempt to interpret material in existing studies in terms of this question. A starting point is Ray's work in Venezuela, which considered how the physical setting of a community and the experiences that residents have had in dealing with one another can affect the level of cohesiveness. This level is likely to be high in communities which are:

1. small, compact, and semi-isolated;

2. built with only one or two entrances, so that people frequently meet one another as they walk in and out;

3. closely knit since their formation, because most of the residents are original settlers who knew one another in an earlier settlement; and

4. characterized by high involvement in community projects, which can generate warmth among neighbors. (Ray 1969:25)

Ray's first two hypotheses stress the effect of the ecological setting on the strength of community. In physical settings where residents are likely to have a high level of interaction, either because the community is small and isolated from other parts of the city or because it is built in a compact, sharply delimited area with a small number of entrances and exits, familiarity develops among the residents. The second two hypotheses concern the previous experiences the residents have had with one another; they suggest that the longer their association and the more rewarding their cooperative experiences, the higher the level of community integration.

In many settings the strength of community is likely to be inversely related to the level of participation of residents in the wider urban society. Ray suggests three conditions that will increase participation in, and integration into, the wider society. First, in areas where employment is high, individuals will maintain a relatively high level of contact outside the community. Furthermore, they will have spending money, which raises their self-esteem and lessens separation between themselves as squatters and other urban dwellers. Second, in small cities bonds are likely to exist between people living in different sections of the city, although such ties are unknown in larger metropolitan areas. Third, allegiance to the city's dominant political party can promote a sense of belonging in the wider society, giving people the feeling that the power structure is "on their side" and that they are vicariously participating in the society (Ray 1969:21).

From Ray's discussion and from our earlier consideration of the creation of squatter settlements in developing countries, a number of variables can be identified which seem to affect the over-all level of political integration in these communities. Patterns of location, employment opportunities, migration experience, political organization, and governmental attitudes and actions all help to shape the level of political integration in a community. Discussion of each of these factors in the literature on squatting aids in the identification of variables to be incorporated into working hypotheses for the analysis of Mathare 2, and in the development of a model for the community formation process among urban squatters.

The variables identified below are separated according to which of the two components of political integration—sense of community or strength of community institutions—they seem to affect most directly. Because sense of community and institutional strength are positively related, variables affecting changes in the level of one should also be related to the other. In some cases the independent variable is clearly seen to be more closely associated with either sense of community or institutional strength, while in other cases the decision is more difficult. As the hypotheses are formulated, the independent variables are associated with the dependent variable where their effect should be greatest. However, it is recognized that any independent variable may be related to the other dependent variable at the same time, and each hypothesis could be restated to reflect this relationship.

Sense of community

1. *The greater the perceived importance of the community in people's lives, the greater the sense of community.*

Sense of community refers to the extent to which members see their community as distinctive and come to agree that common problems need to be resolved peacefully. Although existing studies of squatters do not consider sense of community directly, there are some indirect ways in which they help to explain it. Sense of community should be a function of the importance of the community in people's lives and the distinctiveness of the community from the standpoint of the wider society. Thus, the fewer alternatives people have for achieving goals which are important to them, and the more the community is associated with these goals, the more important the community will be in their lives, and the greater the sense of community they will hold. In Turner's scheme, the community should be of greater importance to the consolidator than to the bridgeheader or status-seeker, because the consolidator finds that his major demands and concerns—the desire for permanent ownership and security of tenure—are most intimately tied to the success or failure of the community, while the other two types of settlers hold goals which are more separate from the community.

2. *Threats to community membership or participation which are moderate in strength should increase sense of community, while the absence of threat or the presence of extremely high levels of threat should be associated with a weaker sense of community.*

Sense of community is fostered when residents find that their own personal goals are tied to the future of the community. The reason for this may be either external or internal to the area. Thus, stigmatization or identification of the squatters as undesirable by outsiders will tend to heighten their sense of common identity. Similarly, threats to community membership or participation can heighten the extent to which squatters perceive that they share a common fate. As was noted above, however, threat can be so overpowering that squatters are demoralized or traumatized, as they come to feel that no amount of organizational effort will be successful.

3. *The greater the number and strength of highly affective symbols uniquely associated with the community, the greater the sense of community.*

4. The higher the level of participation in specific social or political rituals and other community activities, the stronger the sense of community.

An internal force increasing the sense of community can be the development of distinctive, highly affective symbols, such as particular leaders, demands, or successes which are closely associated with a community and which become a focal point for the attention of residents. High levels of participation in community activities should also be associated with increased community identification. Examples of participation may range from a dramatic common experience, such as invasion or work on a community building, to the day-to-day willingness to accept locally established regulations. Both symbolization and participation help people to see the commmunity as distinctive and as relatively important in working toward the solution of particular problems. Participation in community activities is especially important when the resulting experiences are pleasant and rewarding. In competitive or threatening situations, however, people may develop negative feelings about the community, and participation may in fact lead to a diminished sense of community identification.[5]

Strength of institutions

The strength of community institutions is the second element in the definition of political integration. It refers to the range of tasks and the perceived effectiveness of community institutions. In some areas, such as many urban neighborhoods, there are virtually no community-wide institutions, while in other locations people may participate in a wide range and number, both formal and informal. The presence or absence, as well

5. Striking cases where participation may be related to the development of negative feelings could include slavery or other situations of strong compulsion or high competition.

as the perceived effectiveness, of community institutions is related to the distinctiveness or homogeneity of the population of a community, to the level of mutual interdependence which develops within the community, and to the flexibility of its institutions and the talents of its leaders.

5. *The higher the social and cultural homogeneity of a community, the stronger community institutions will be.*

Social and cultural homogeneity is often an important basis for community organization efforts. People coming from a particular background or sharing other characteristics, ranging from religious beliefs to socioeconomic status, are often drawn to work together. A distinctive way of life, which separates community members from the wider society, may refer to many common shared experiences—previous residence, mutual participation in a political or social movement, or common ethnicity.[6]

6. *The greater the proportion of interactions taking place within a community, the stronger community institutions will be.*

7. *The higher the level of mutual interdependence within a community, the stronger community institutions will be.*

A second source of pressure toward the development of community institutions is the extent to which residents are highly dependent on one another, and the extent to which they engage in a high level of social interaction within the community. As both Ray and Turner note, interaction is likely when relatively few residents work outside the community and when day-to-day activities require mutual assistance and cooperation. In such

6. The level of social and cultural homogeneity is clearly one variable which contributes to the development of a sense of community as well as to institutional development, and is the independent variable which was most difficult to place with a particular dependent variable.

situations people are more likely to create institutions to serve their common needs. Thus a community in which the government provides no social services may develop local organizations to handle problems such as education or sanitation. Residents come to realize that such problems cannot be solved solely on the individual level, but at the same time they have relatively little hope that the government will act. In contrast, when government recognition brings with it social services and security of land tenure, the mutual needs of community members are handled from outside.

8. *The greater the institutional generalizability, or spillover potential, the stronger community institutions will be.*

The flexibility of local institutions and the skills of local leaders also determine the strength of community institutions. Some institutions are narrow in purpose and appear incapable of task expansion, while in other cases the spillover potential is quite large. The more generalizable a community's institutions, the easier it should be to strengthen those institutions. Institutional generalizability is a function of an attitudinal predisposition within a community—an acceptance or rejection of the notion that the tasks which community institutions perform must be carefully spelled out and that they are relatively difficult to change.

9. *The greater the level of the leaders' skills, both task-related and social-emotional, the stronger community institutions will be.*

The skills of leaders are crucial in determining the success with which community institutions operate. Leadership skills can be classified as either social-emotional or task skills (Bales 1950; Danielski 1961). While there are sometimes leaders who serve as both social-emotional and task leaders in a community or organization, the most typical pattern is one in which these two functions are divided among several leaders. The social-emotional leader is particularly important in developing loyalty to a community, and in impressing people with the urgency of supporting community institutions. The task leader, on the other hand, plays a crucial role in dealing with particular substantive problems. He knows what to do and how to do it, and his skills are necessary for long-term success. The viability of community institutions is tied to his ability to solve the real, day-to-day problems confronting people.

Local community integration

Finally, there are several variables which appear to be important for understanding the degree of integration in squatter settlements in terms of the small size and local character of such communities.

10. *The smaller the community, and the greater the proportion of interactions which are face to face, the higher the level of community integration.*[7]

Local communities which are small in size are often integrated through direct, unmediated interpersonal ties between community members. Communications through the media can be ignored or selectively perceived; this is more difficult in situations of face-to-face contact.

11. *The higher the level of isolation, the higher the level of political integration in a community.*

Community autonomy also affects the level of integration, as residents are likely to develop greater ties to one another

7. In this and the next proposition the dependent variable is political integration as a whole, rather than either of its two components, sense of community and institutional strength.

in situations where the community is relatively isolated from the wider society. Thus Turner suggests that in Latin America squatter settlements in the most peripheral parts of the metropolitan region and those on the least valuable land are the most likely to improve, and Ray also suggests that relative isolation should be associated with community cohesiveness.

Conclusions

The literature on squatters provides us with a starting point in understanding the process of community formation in Mathare 2. A number of variables which seem to affect the over-all level of community integration are identified in existing studies. The hypotheses developed in this chapter will organize the analysis of Mathare 2. First, however, we need to examine briefly the social and political context in which Mathare 2 is located—that of Kenya's capital city, Nairobi.

5

Urban growth and squatters in Nairobi

Nairobi is a relatively new African city whose population has quadrupled to more than 500,000 in the last twenty years.[1] Prior to European penetration into Kenya, the land on which the city is located was a marsh which served as a natural border between the Kikuyu population of Kiambu, to the north, and the Athi Plains, controlled by the Masai, to the south. Building in the city began in 1899 when the railway from Mombasa, heading for Uganda, reached Nairobi (Political Record Book 1899: 4). In the early years health conditions in the marshland provoked several battles over the site of the city, but railway officials protested vigorously enough so that it was not changed (Parker 1949:259). By 1906, when Nairobi boasted a population of more than 13,000, the railway and government headquarters were moved there from Mombasa.

From the outset the population was stratified by race, and each racial tier contained numerous subdivisions. The Europeans dominated the government and the larger financial institutions of the city, although they never made up more than 8 to 10 per cent of the population; the Asians, who had first come to

1. In 1969 the population of the city was 509,286, a fourfold increase from the 1948 census. A part of the increase is attributable to an expansion of the boundaries of the city in the early 1960s, but most of it is due to migration to the city.

East Africa in large numbers to work on the construction of the railway, were soon chiefly engaged in all ranges of commerce or as artisans, and made up about a quarter of the city's population; the remaining two-thirds of the residents of Nairobi were Africans who worked in the most menial occupations.[2] The three racial groups were separated residentially and were stratified socially as well as economically. For example, until the independence era, differential wage scales for the same work existed for each race in most areas of employment. The Europeans maintained firm political control, although there were often bitter conflicts between the administration and the settler community (Bennett 1963).

Africans did not generally regard Nairobi as a suitable site for permanent residence. As a result there was a high turnover in employment, a relative scarcity of women and children in the urban population, and frequent movement between the city and the rural areas. Social conditions during the colonial period made life unattractive to Africans. Wages were at a subsistence level, there was a color bar, and housing was inadequate for family living (Forrester 1962). Between 1940 and 1960 only two housing estates (neighborhoods)—Kaloleni and Ziwani—were constructed with the specific intention of providing housing facilities for African families. Yet even in these estates some of the units were only single rooms, and the estates could accommodate only a small proportion of the city's African residents.

Since Nairobi's founding, a pattern has developed according to which men migrate to the city to obtain employment, leave their families in the rural areas, and make periodic visits home. The duration of the visits depends on the distance of an individual's home from the city, as well as on his ability to finance the journey. At a minimum, most men try to spend their month's leave in the rural areas each year. It is incorrect to categorize

2. The African proportion of the population has risen faster than the Asian or European. In 1969 the African population of the city was 421,079 (83 per cent), Asians totaled 67,189 (13 per cent), and Europeans 19,185 (4 per cent).

such persons simply as target workers, because in many cases they view their move to the city in long-range terms, rather than simply as a means of obtaining the money for one or two items, such as land or a brideprice. The increasing desire on the part of Kenyans to educate their children means that a continuing source of cash income is essential. Thus a man can foresee leaving urban employment only if he has a job in another part of the country, perhaps as a laborer on a European farm, or unless all his children have been educated and all his sons married.[3]

The city and thresholds in the social life cycle

Very few adults living in Nairobi were born there. Interviews with samples of the population in Shauri Moyo and Kariokor, two Nairobi neighborhoods, elicited data showing that only 20 of the 498 adults (4 per cent) were born in the city.[4] Their average length of residence in the city is 9.6 years, and on the average they have spent 29 per cent of their lives in the city. The census data show that the age structure of the Nairobi population is clustered around the 20–40 age group to a greater extent than is the population of the country as a whole.

Kenyans do not consider Nairobi a desirable place to celebrate major thresholds in the social life cycle—birth, initiation, marriage, and death. While initiation ceremonies, such as circumcision rituals, are often performed in the city, there is a definite preference for holding them in the rural areas whenever possible. In part this feeling is due to the greater control which the police exert over city residents; in part it is due to a certain degree of self-consciousness concerning traditional ceremonies and ritu-

3. Greater detail on life styles in the city and rural-urban contacts in Kenya is found in Ross (forthcoming).
4. Details concerning the composition and characteristics of this sample, which furnished data for this entire section, are found in Ross (1968).

als in tribally mixed areas of the city (the Kikuyu are over-whelmingly in the majority in those areas of the city where, to the author's knowledge, Kikuyu circumcision ceremonies are performed); and in part it is due to the desire to conduct them on one's own land.

The same attitude prevails regarding marriage and death. Most marriages take place outside the city. Data from one pretest showed that 84 per cent of the married individuals in the sample reported that they were married outside Nairobi (Ross 1968: 80). A related characteristic is the low proportion of intertribal marriages; marriages taking place in the rural areas are almost invariably intratribal. Only about 10 per cent of the married individuals (35 out of 346) reported that their spouse was not from their tribe.

Nairobi is not considered "good" place to get married, par-tially because Nairobi is not a "good" place to find a wife. The older generation suspects that a single woman living in the city is by definition a prostitute. Men are often reluctant to marry women they meet in the city because they are afraid that such women will be too independent and thus uncontrollable. They realize that a woman who has lived in the city for several years may not look kindly on the idea of living alone with her children on her husband's small plot of land while he stays in the city. Whenever young unmarried men in the city are asked if they would prefer to marry a woman from the city or one from the rural areas, they choose a woman from the country.

Nairobi is not the location a man would choose for his death, either. Most individuals make plans to leave the city after their productive years are over, or as soon as it is no longer possible to find employment. This is reflected in the high level of contact with the rural areas. Only 3 per cent of the adults in the city are over the age of 50, and only 16 per cent are over 40. Burial societies, on the scale which some authors describe in West African cities, are not found in Nairobi. In case of death in Nairobi, the body of the deceased is usually sent to the rural area from which he came.[5] There are some forms of burial insurance available to cover the cost of body shipment, but a much more prevalent practice is the taking of a spontaneous collection by an individual's relatives and close friends to raise the money when a death occurs unexpectedly in Nairobi.

Land and security

Thus far, most Kenyans have shown reluctance to commit themselves permanently to urban life. Men will usually invest money in land in the rural areas before they will spend it on a house or business in the city. This is explained as "security," and is expressed in terms of a "low-risk" strategy. Men argue that if they die, their wives can quickly spend cash that is left or lose a business through mismanagement, but they can always live on the *shamba* (farm) and plant enough to support the children. "If the political climate changes," they argue; "if I lose my job"; "if we have bad times here again. . . ." In each of these cases, land is considered more important than a house or business in the city, because with even a small land holding an individual can at least manage to survive, if not to prosper.

One important constraint to the purchase of land for men working in the city is the burden placed on them to pay school fees for their children. These days, at least among the major agricultural tribes of the country—the Kikuyu, Kamba, Meru, Kisii, Baluhya, and Luo—there is great pressure for education. Children want to attend school and parents want to send them. Within Nairobi, the City Education Department asserts that there is a space in school for every child who presents himself with the fees, although in other parts of the country this is not always true. Education is often viewed as the same sort of investment in the future as the purchase of land. A man who is able to

5. A dramatic example of this was seen following the assassination of Tom Mboya, minister for economic development and planning, in 1969. Despite the fact that Mboya had spent almost his entire life in Nairobi, he was taken to be buried in South Nyanza, on the island in Lake Victoria where he was born.

see his son obtain a secondary school certificate or a higher degree knows that the child will assume some (if not most) of the responsibility for the education of his younger siblings and that he will take care of his parents as they grow older. This may mean, for example, that a father will deliberately forego the purchase of land in order to educate his son, in the hope that once his son has obtained a higher degree he will purchase land on which his parents can reside.

Residential zones and land use

Throughout Nairobi's history, land use has been closely regulated.[6] During the colonial period, residential areas for the African, Asian, and European communities were carefully demarcated. Furthermore, in the major African residential zones in Eastlands, the residents were most frequently renters, living in housing built either by the City Council or by their employers. Consequently, on the surface most African neighborhoods in Nairobi lack spontaneity and seem sterile in comparison with those in other cities on the continent.

The majority of the African population during the early decades of Nairobi's history lived in three estates to the east of the center-city area: Pangani, Kariokor, and Pumwani. Pangani, located where Ngara Road runs today, originally housed better-paid Africans, but by the 1930s it reportedly deteriorated. It was finally destroyed in 1938 and replaced by Shauri Moyo (Parker 1949:81). Kariokor, built by the government in 1928, consisted of 950 tiny dormitory-style rooms and derived its name from the fact that it was located on the site of the camp for the "Carrier Corps" during World War I. It was finally destroyed in the early 1960s and replaced by a dozen four-story buildings containing three-bedroom flats. Pumwani estate, opened in 1921, contained mud and wattle houses owned exclusively by Arabs

6. A more complete description of the geographical zones in Nairobi, and particularly in Eastlands, is found in McVicar (1969).

and Asians in the early years, although ownership later shifted to Africans. It was the largest African area, and was severely overcrowded. Part of the neighborhood still stood in 1970, although the government is in the process of replacing it with expensive modern housing.

With the population growing more rapidly in the last thirty years, the government built additional housing estates at a faster rate. Some, such as Shauri Moyo, Bahati, and Ofafa I (Kunguni), were made up only of single rooms, often shared by several men. Others, such as Ziwani and Kaloleni, represented early attempts to provide several rooms per dwelling, although these were very small in size. By 1960, with independence imminent, the government finally began to build several estates with apartments in which a man could live with his family. Among these are the Ofafa estates, the new Kariokor, Uhuru, and Woodley, which is located in the western part of the city.

Increasing stratification of the African population by education, occupation, and income, combined with the general population growth in the independence period, produced a greater dispersion of Africans in the city. The areas of Eastleigh, Nairobi West, and Nairobi South, formerly Asian neighborhoods, now have large African populations. There are also many Africans living in the formerly European areas. Additional population growth has been absorbed through increased crowding in the existing African areas of the city. Despite the fact that the government is building at a faster rate than ever, it does not come close to housing a population growing at about 6 or 7 per cent a year.

One response to population pressure is the growing proportion of the population living in uncontrolled or squatter settlements. In some cases, such as in Kamakunji or the Quarry Road area, the government has moved in and burned out squatters' houses whenever they have appeared. In other locations, such as Mathare Valley or Langata, they have chosen to regulate existing squatters and to limit the number of new houses built in the area. Squatter settlements in Nairobi attract very different individuals than do the newer housing estates. In general, the squatter is poorer, is less likely to have a job, and lacks the skills needed to escape from the marginal existence he leads in the city.

Location and settlement of Mathare Valley

Mathare Valley is populated by urban misfits and rural outcasts in the sense that these individuals lack the skills and abilities needed to participate in the modern economy of Nairobi, while at the same time they have no meaningful rural alternative to life in the city. Within this context, they are forced to live in a community such as Mathare, where it is possible to eke out a marginal existence; for despite the fact that the village is physically separated from the rest of the city and is a negative symbol to most people, it is not isolated in terms of social interactions. The location of this village, like that of many squatter communities, is a function of its interdependence with the outside. Situated near the police barracks, an Air Force base, a mental hospital, and the neighborhood of Eastleigh, Mathare is well placed to provide a large number of people with liquid refreshment and entertainment at a low price. It is also located close enough to other sections of Nairobi to allow residents to go to the markets, travel to work, or visit friends and family.

Mathare Valley was the home of about 15,000 squatters in 1968,[7] although in 1960 there was almost no one living in the area. In the late 1940s and early 1950s the settlement in the Mathare River area was a center of Kikuyu unrest and ferment. During part of this time arms were stored in the area, and there were politically motivated murders and beatings. Soon after the declaration of the State of Emergency in Kenya, in 1952, the

7. This is an extremely conservative estimate, a great deal lower than the estimates of the City Council and the National Christian Council of Kenya in the next few years.

colonial government moved into the Mathare area with bulldozers and destroyed all the squatter housing.

> On the morning of the 17th April [1953], a cordon of Police and Military was placed round two of the illegal settlements in the Mathare Valley. All of the occupants of the houses were taken in front of screening teams and this resulted in the arrest of several hundred men, who were wanted in their own reserves. The houses themselves were searched for weapons, one shotgun and two pistols being recovered. Some 600 men and about 400 women were subsequently released, and after they recovered their property from the houses, ordered to leave the village. . . . The villages in the Mathare Valley were subsequently demolished, on Sunday the 19th April. On the morning of the 20th April, a Police Officer discovered the body of an African in Mabarani [in the area between Mathare Village 4 today and Kariobangi] and a search revealed a total of 12 bodies. The effect of the arrival of a force of police to make this search was the signal for the complete evacuation of the whole village, and by nightfall all the inhabitants had left. The area having been scheduled for evacuation, the houses were demolished the following day. . . . On April 25th, the illegal village of Kariobangi just outside the City Council boundary was cordoned off and after screening, occupants of the houses were ordered to leave, and the entire village was demolished. (Nairobi City Council 1953)

Many residents of the Mathare Valley area spent much of the next seven years in detention camps and under other restrictions on the basis of real or imagined connections with the Mau Mau freedom fighters.[8] By 1961, when the State of Emergency had officially ended, many of Mathare's former residents began returning to Nairobi in the hope of finding work. Housing and jobs were scarce then, as they are today, and people lacking the necessary skills to find employment, as well as those unable to find accommodations elsewhere, moved into Mathare, where both a small income and housing could be obtained. Some found

8. Throughout this period the colonial government rigidly controlled population movements in this area, not permitting any settlement at all.

they could earn enough to live on through brewing beer, prostitution, or small-scale agriculture. Others became landlords, letting out rooms in the mud and wattle houses which were cheaply and quickly constructed. Some started small provision stores and other shops which catered to the needs of the area residents. Finally, there were people who held jobs outside the valley, on either a permanent or a temporary basis, and who lived in Mathare because of its low cost or its location. Since the early 1960s the rapid population growth of the area has always reflected the severe housing shortage in other parts of Nairobi. The destruction of the old Kariokor contributed significantly to the early growth of Mathare, as did the destruction of Pumwani during the time of this study, several years later.

By 1967, the Mathare Valley area was divided into four major squatter settlements, each with its own leaders and social characteristics. The first three villages each contain about 1,000 mud and wattle houses tightly packed together. There are open spaces between the villages, which are located on the southern side of the Mathare River. Village 4, situated on the other side of the river, is much smaller, having only about 75 houses spread over a relatively wide area. Most of the houses in Village 4 have a small piece of land, which the residents farm intensively. Stone quarries next to Village 4 also provide work for about 75 to 100 men in the area. There are three other small settlements located between Mathare Village 4 and Kariobangi to the east, called Ngei 1, Ngei 2, and Ngei 3 after a prominent Kamba politician, Paul Ngei.

This study considers only Village 2, which is smaller than Village 3, larger than Village 4, and about the same size as Village 1. During the period of the study, it was the best-organized village, and its leaders appeared to be more efficient, less corrupt, and more popular than those in any other village. It is also much more tribally homogeneous than Village 3, for example. Despite these differences, the social and economic conditions of the people living in each of the first three villages were practically identical. All were dependent on the *pombe* (beer) economy, and individuals lived with continual threats of arrest for their illegal activities and of removal because they were squatters on private land.

Political responses to squatters and squatting

The rapid expansion of Nairobi and the coming of political independence in the mid-1960s meant that the burden of housing, jobs, and social services for the urban population fell on a new group of Kenya politicians and administrators who replaced the senior British colonial rulers. Their initial response was the continuation of policies that had existed in the late colonial period, the construction of more family-type dwellings, and the use of permanent materials such as concrete blocks. Their response toward squatters was nonrecognition and denial of the problem.

Led by prominent politicians, including the president, the public developed the attitude that squatters and other unemployed groups in the city should "go back to the land" and contribute to economic development through their agricultural abilities. Of course, this attitude assumed that they had land to go back to—an assumption which was usually unfounded. At the same time, the government apparently adopted a dual policy toward squatters in Nairobi, permitting them to settle in areas such as Mathare and Langata, but periodically removing them from Kamakunji, Kaburini, Quarry Road, and other areas that were either close to the center of the city or clearly visible from major roads. A commissioner of squatters was appointed; with the district commissioner, the chief administrative officer of the central government, he was responsible for limiting and regulating squatter settlements.

The City Council of Nairobi, faced with the problem of building and administering most of the public housing in the city, realized that the gap between the housing demand and their ability to supply dwellings was increasing yearly. They began to explore alternatives to the expensive housing estates, which were based on a British town-planning model. The earliest experiment was Kariobangi, a "site-and-service" scheme in the northeastern part of the city, near the Eastleigh Air Force Base. The Council established roads, water points, and latrines; then it rented plots to individuals, who had to promise to live in the area. Many renters were squatters who had been removed from areas nearer the center of Nairobi. Each plot was large enough for a small house with four rooms, and typically the renter of the plot lived in one room and found tenants for the other three.

Within a short period of time, houses built of mud and wattle appeared on almost every plot. Many of the plot-renters disappeared, however; some sold their plots for a few hundred shillings to enterprising businessmen, while others found a relative to live in one of the rooms and to "manage" the house for them. Many complained that Kariobangi was too far away from the industrial area or center city, and that the bus fare to work was more than they could afford. Others could not find work in Nairobi at all, and returned to their rural families. This relatively large-scale exodus of the orginal plot-renters disturbed the City Council planners and indicated to many that the site-and-service scheme in Kariobangi was a failure. Others, however, stressed the monetary savings. Since the residents supplied the capital for construction and for improvements on the houses, the total cost per housing unit in Kariobangi was a fraction of what it would have been if the Council had undertaken the total construction itself. Furthermore, despite the exodus of the orginal plot-renters from Kariobangi, more people moved into the area each year, and the net population increased. Significantly, the quality of the houses steadily improved as more and more people put better roofs on their houses, added cement floors, and built thicker walls, often using cement blocks. By 1970 there were a number of small shops in Kariobangi, and the area clearly provided evidence that the government could help direct urban growth without having to pay its entire cost.

The site-and-service scheme is intended to provide managed growth at low cost. The problem of what to do with squatters already living on land that is not their own presents a very different problem to the government. From the time of independence until 1970 both the Kenya and Nairobi governments treated squatter communities as foreign countries, giving them de facto, but not de jure, recognition. They sought the cooperation of squatter leaders in limiting growth of the community and in handling other problems, but at the same time refused to provide any social services in the area. When the residents of Mathare 2 collected money to pay for water pipes and a meter, the city government refused even to sell them water on the grounds that the settlement was illegal. The politicians and administrators still held to the belief that if the squatters were not encouraged in any way, many of them would decide to leave the city and go back to the land.

When the major part of this study ended in March, 1968, the main evidence of the likelihood of changes in government policy was based on the high interest of City Council planners and other administrators in the problems of Mathare, and in their recognition that some alternative to the costly government financing of housing in the city needed to be found. In the few years following 1968, spurred by developments in the Mathare area and by the increased realization on the part of prominent politicians that squatters would not simply "go back to the land," government policy changed sharply. Under the impetus of the Town Planning Department and interested outsiders, mainly in the National Christian Council of Kenya, the city began to outline programs to develop unoccupied land in the Mathare-Kariobangi area and to improve housing and social services such as roads, sewers, schools, health centers, and recreation facilities in already occupied squatter areas. Thus not only would the threat of physical removal from the area be lifted, but assistance would be given in meeting many of the major problems that squatters face. At the same time, the government was concerned with, but less sure about how to attack, the problems of jobs and employment.

The most visible changes in the Mathare area between March, 1968, and May, 1970, when we returned to Kenya for a short visit, resulted from private initiative rather than from changes in government policy. Late in 1969 land-buying companies began purchasing and developing plots in the Mathare area. Some of these plots were empty, while others were occupied by Mathare squatters. At first it seemed that Mathare residents were involved in the land-development schemes; however, it soon became clear that most of the developers were not squatters but wealthier entrepreneurs, many from Kiambu, who saw a chance to make a high profit at a relatively low risk. On the empty land, the developers began building four-room wooden houses with cement floors and sheet-metal roofs at a cost of about fifteen hundred shillings. Each room rented for at least a hundred shillings a month, so a developer could get his capital back in four months.

Developers purchasing occupied land were of two types: companies which had no conflict with the population residing on their plots, and which planned to develop new housing for the current residents; and companies which had bought land occupied by large nonmember populations and had submitted development plans calling for the demolition of existing housing and the construction of new housing sufficient for members.[9] The latter agitated for the removal of nonmembers, but the government promised Mathare Valley squatters that they would not be removed until the government found permanent housing for them. Their plots are all in the eastern section of the Mathare area and are located in Villages 1, 2, and 3.

Forced by the land companies on the one hand and the plan-

9. These distinctions are taken from a short paper, "Mathare Valley: Paper No. 2," Nairobi, November, 1969, which outlines developments in land-buying cooperatives and policy options open to the city government at that time.

ners on the other, the city government moved by 1970 toward a comprehensive policy for the Mathare Valley area which included the development of site-and-service schemes on unoccupied land in the western part of the area, the purchase of occupied land from plot-holders, and the provision of a minimum level of social services in the area. The major limitations, of course, are financial, and it is not clear how much the city will actually be able to pay for. Furthermore, without a radical change in the job market, the squatters will continue to be dependent on their illegal beer brewing and other subsistence activities outlined in greater detail below.

The main concern of our inquiry, however, rests in the earlier period, prior to the intensive governmental and private interest in Mathare Valley, and the ways in which the inhabitants created and developed a wide range of community institutions to handle problems too large for individuals and to help provide for the peaceful resolution of disputes. The effect of the changes in the area on the internal organization of the community is indeed an interesting and important question, but not the major one of this study.

6

Political integration in Mathare 2

Political integration has both an attitudinal component, the sense of community, and an institutional component, the strength of the community's institutions. We expect these two components to be positively related; the greater the task load and the more effective a community's institutions are in producing regularized, peaceful management of community problems, the stronger the sense of community is likely to be. Conversely, the stronger common sentiments are, the more likely community institutions will be to take on additional tasks and to be seen as effective.

What is less clear is the sequential order in which these interactions are likely to take place. Is institutional development likely to take place only after common identification exists? Or is the successful establishment of institutions likely to precede a heightened sense of community? A tentative answer to these questions is that integration has a better chance of succeeding when institutions and sense of community develop together, although the evidence is not without ambiguity.

Nye (1971:48–54) outlines three different positions on this question. The federalist position stresses institutional integration as a first step which leads to the development of common sentiments, policy integration, and a secure community. The functionalist position aims at the integration of policy-making, which leads to the development of a secure community; institutional and attitudinal integration are unimportant in this position. The neofunctionalist position also begins with the aim of achieving high integration of policy-making in functionally specific areas, but this position recognizes that at least a moderate level of institutional integration is also needed to lead to an increased sense of community and, finally, to higher levels of institutional cooperation and the growth of a secure community. While there are certainly differences between these three positions, what all of them share is the conviction that cooperation in broad institutional or functionally specific policy areas is a step which precedes changes in attitudes and the development of a common sense of identity as a community.

Others, such as Deutsch and his students, have tended to argue the opposite position, that integration is most likely when a sense of community precedes institutional development. In one of the clearest cases, Merritt (1966), who analyzed the press in colonial America, showed that there was a significant change in orientation away from England and toward other colonies in the forty years preceding the American Revolution. He found that growth of community sentiments was cyclical and at a high level *before* the Stamp Act and other Intolerable Acts in the 1760s, and that it clearly preceded the development of common political institutions. The presence of a sense of community appeared to be a precondition to the development of a common response to the English government and to the creation of American political institutions. Nonetheless, it should also be noted that the common institutions created in the 1770s were far weaker than the American institutions established in 1787 at the Constitutional Convention and in the subsequent 175 years. Thus, while sense of community seemed to precede initial institutional growth, later institutional strengthening seemed at least partially a function of increasing community identity. In short, there is considerable feedback between the two variables, and, as the neofunctionalists suggest, increases in either one are likely to be highly related to increases in the other.

Although sense of community and institutional development should be positively interrelated, it is important to develop different indicators for each. Rather than relying on a single indicator of political integration, "a more fruitful approach is to break apart the concept of integration, develop concrete measurements for all its component parts and leave the relationship between them open for empirical verification" (Nye 1971:26). In this study of Mathare 2 we will attempt to follow Nye's suggestion, at the same time recognizing that in an inductive study where descriptive materials are interpreted retrospectively in terms of theoretical categories, the necessary data are not always available.

What follows is an account of the formal political structures in Mathare 2 which permits us to develop direct and indirect measures of the two components of political integration as well as to give the reader a clearer understanding of the range of community problems considered. While there were six distinct institutions in Mathare 2, it should be mentioned that the key political leaders do not place great importance on institutional differences, and that the functional specificity of each institution is more important in this description than in day-to-day operations.

Community organizations and projects

Since pre-independence days, the village leaders have expanded the village committee to the point where it now oversees the operation of six community-wide institutions. A discussion of each of them will explain the kinds of tasks that the village leaders have undertaken, and how the operation of these institutions contributes to the over-all political integration of the community. Each institution is discussed in terms of the functions attributed to it by the village leaders, and the reader should remember that the separation of tasks often does not take place in practice.

The village committee

In theory, the village committee, headed by the chairman, is the highest authority in the community. It makes rules regulating behavior in the community, organizes village projects, and raises money to carry them out. The committee, made up of eleven men and eleven women, holds several meetings a month for committee members and public meetings about once every five or six weeks. Neither the committee meetings nor the public meetings are characterized by a great deal of give and take. Rather, the chairman presents information or ideas, and there is little reaction or comment on the part of others present.

The chairman, Kiboro, is the center of any meeting when he is present. His personal dynamism and his control of a wide range of social facts make him the dominant figure in any community group. Similarly, while other people participate in village committee meetings as well as in general public meetings, it is Kiboro who decides when they will talk, how long they will speak, and whether they will be praised or rebuked for their remarks. He thoroughly enjoys speaking to crowds, and has mastered the art of political rhetoric. Any of the meetings held in the village are therefore characterized by different sorts of remarks which Kiboro might make, and which are not equally literal in their intent.

The notes of a typical general village meeting presented in Figure 6.1 show that many statements communicate information to the people, such as the fact that the new water supply is installed and ready for use. A second theme reflects the aspirations of the village leaders and many of the people in the community. For example, at several meetings Kiboro discussed various land-purchasing schemes in the Nairobi area that the community might consider. In addition, Kiboro used the public meetings to communicate threats to village groups which he felt were opposed to his leadership. He often threatened shopkeepers who did not close their *duka* during public meetings. He used the public meeting to denounce "individuals" who accused the leaders of mismanagement of funds, continually challenging them to furnish proof of their charges. A related purpose of the public meeting is to deliver a certain amount of political rhetoric and social advice, although this is usually stated without enough conviction to make much difference. For example, from time to time Kiboro would solemnly tell everyone in the village that drinking was a bad thing and that it was giving the village a bad name. At other times he made threats that were obviously unenforceable and that he had no real intention of trying to enforce. In the meeting cited, for example, he announced that anyone not helping to build the village nursery school would have to pay a five-shilling fine, but this was not enforced.

FIGURE 6.1 MINUTES OF THE GENERAL VILLAGE MEETING, MATHARE VILLAGE 2, OCTOBER 9, 1967

1. Kiboro opened the meeting asking the people of the village to support the government of His Excellency the President Mzee Jomo Kenyatta and said that everyone should work together in the spirit of Harambee.

2. He announced that there are over 2,000 people and 60 traders living in Village 2 now.

3. The new water supply is now installed and ready for use.

4. He said that people should take care of making repairs on their houses. Also, people should not brew beer inside their houses and keep large amounts of beer there, because if they do the district officer will come and destroy their houses.

5. He pointed out that many people tell lies about drinking. They say such things as village money or social hall monies have been misspent. He then challenged them to come forward with any evidence that they had.

6. Everyone in the village must pay the Sh. 1/- for the monthly youth

wing subscription. If people fail to pay to support the youth wing, no one will be able to attend to their complaints.

7. He said that many people failed to register to vote and if people are found without voting cards they will be heavily punished.

8. Kiboro stated that some people in the village drink too much, and he threatened that if they don't cut down he wouldn't intervene with the police and they would have to face the consequences themselves.

9. He told the people who own the small shops to be more careful about their drinking, because otherwise they could ruin their business.

10. He told the people that when they get into trouble they realize how he helps them, but if they fail to cooperate in the village, then he wouldn't do anything for them. "We must get together to cooperate to build. For example, we can boycott a bad person or shop together and have an effect."

11. People were told that they should send all their children to the nursery school because now the city schools are beginning to take children who have studied first in the Mathare nursery school.

12. Everyone who wants to buy shares in the social hall is welcome to do so. Also, those people who want to withdraw may do so.

13. People were told to rebuild their houses if they have been authorized to do so.

14. If people still don't understand the system of water charges then they should speak to a member of the committee and he will explain it.

15. The President, Mzee Jomo Kenyatta, will speak at Kamakunji on October 20, Kenyatta Day, and everyone from the village must go and hear him.

16. There will be a meeting of the cooperative society on November 5, and a meeting of the members of the social hall on October 29.

17. He warned the people not to continue to spread bad rumors and also not to fight with each other.

18. The people of the village should respect Kenyatta Day. They should be polite, not drink and not make trouble.

19. He told them that on the 24th Dick Bancroft was going to come to the village and show movies.

20. The leader of the youth wing spoke and said that it was a lie that the new nursery school would be finished because whenever he sends the youth wingers to call the public to work, they don't turn up. Then he asked the public to pay the Sh. 1/- youth wing subscription and told them that they must respect the youth wing.

21. The vice-chairman, Kariuki Gichohi, said that everyone should make sure that their children are in the nursery school and that the public worked hard to finish it.

22. Kiboro said that if a house is found where there is Nubian Gin, it will be demolished. Also, if traders are found stocking stolen goods in their shop, it will be destroyed.

23. People in the village should not abuse the youth wing, because their cooperation is needed.

24. If a man is a member of the social hall, and he doesn't help to build the nursery school, his child will be charged a Shs. 5/- school fee.

The general village meetings are an important vehicle for communication between the village leaders and the community. They stress the formal aspects of the leadership roles in the village, as committee members usually are seated apart from nonmembers. Furthermore, they provide evidence that the leaders are busily working on various village problems and allow them to present their solutions. Finally, they stress the ability of the leader to operate in the wider political context of Nairobi, as outside visitors often are present at general village meetings and are invited to say a few words. Invariably, whether they are administrators such as district officers or visitors from the university, they tell the crowd that they are very impressed with the self-help projects they have seen in the village and that they think Kiboro and the other leaders are doing a good job.

The meetings of the village committee, in contrast to the general village meetings, usually deal with much more technical problems and serve more as a vehicle of decision-making than the general meetings, which are primarily used to announce decisions that have already been made. In the committee meetings Kiboro, and sometimes other members, presents ideas which are discussed and then perhaps passed in the form of resolutions. (See Figure 6.2.) Although in fact Kiboro makes most decisions and then presents them to the committee, he feels that it is necessary to have their approval and support when he introduces his ideas to the wider community. The committee is not a mere rubber stamp, however, as he often has to argue for a long time before a consensus is reached; other committee members are not shy about presenting their points of view.

FIGURE 6.2 MINUTES OF VILLAGE COMMITTEE MEETING, AUGUST 22, 1967

1. Nyokabi was told by the chairman that she could build a house in the village, but she is still living in the youth wing house. Kiboro told her to leave the house; they exchanged bad words, and then he hit her. She had been told to leave by the end of July, but the youth wing leader said that despite the fact that she had given Kiboro money to buy the posts for building her house they were not delivered yet. Therefore, she refused to leave the youth wing house. If a person was not a member of the youth wing, Kiboro said he would have to pay rent to the community. In addition, the committee requested everyone in debt to Kiboro to pay him by Thursday because he had to pay back the money for the building materials used for the youth wing house.

2. Kiboro said that the youth wing houses were built by the community and belong to everyone in the village. They then passed the following resolutions: (1) Everyone in the youth wing houses from the 1st of September must pay a rent of Shs. 35/- per room if they are not members of the youth wing. (2) The same will be done for the water house. Then they all decided that this must be discussed at the next meeting, and that anyone dissatisfied with their decision could file a court case.

3. A man was put in charge of selling beer in the canteen. He was told to make sure that only people on the list prepared by the committee could sell their beer in the social hall. They also said that many people were bothering him when he was working hard as a leader in the hall and he had many problems to look after.

4. There are nine people working in the hall, four women and five men. Further discussion of beer selling was adjourned until the next meeting when the accounts from the selling could be presented.

5. The system of depositing and withdrawing the youth wing money must be changed because it is too cumbersome.

Problems of the social hall are not separated from other problems that the community leaders consider at their meetings. Thus, during the research period, they made a number of regulations concerning the admission fees for the hall, the regulations that govern beer selling, and the payment of money for food to people working in the hall and on other community projects. Similarly, the committee felt that any community problem was appropriate for consideration: the installation of a new water supply, a fight between several people in the village, or the charge that a member of the youth wing had abused his position and should be dismissed. The social hall, however, occupied most of their attention during the period in which the research was conducted because of the scale of its operations, the number of people involved in its activities, and the revenue that it produced for the community. Therefore, to better understand the work of the village leaders, we will discuss the operation of the social hall in Village 2.

The social hall

The social hall is the largest single building in the village, consisting of one large room for dances and large meetings, the village offices, a room where one of the nursery-school classes and night school are conducted, and several single rooms that are used by people who work for the community. In front of the hall is the only large vacant piece of land in the village, a dirt square about 100 feet by 100 feet, used variously as a playground, meeting place, movie theater, and parking lot.

What makes the hall particularly important is its economic role in the community. Soon after the hall was built, in late

1966, the community purchased a small electric generator which supplied power to run the electric guitars and the lights in the hall, allowing the community to run its own night club. The income to the community came from the admissions to the hall; from beer, soda, food, and cigarettes that were sold at the canteen; and from the fees people paid for the right to sell their own homemade beer in the hall. Initial financing of the hall came from memberships sold in the form of shares to people in the village. In the short run, the income from the hall was important in providing capital for community projects, for paying people's fines, for providing subsistence wages to villagers, and as a tangible sign of village achievements. In the long run, some of the leaders hoped that the hall might earn enough money for the community to allow members to purchase land, either in the city or in the Rift Valley.

By October, 1967, 308 people had paid 10,800 shillings for shares in the social hall. Each member owned between one and five shares, which cost 20 shillings each; people who wished to withdraw their membership were able to get the money they had paid for their shares refunded. The nightly dances provided an additional income of between 6,000 and 7,000 shillings per month during the period when the research was conducted. Some nights the revenue was as high as 550 shillings, while on others it was less than 100 shillings. The crucial variable was the time of the month. Salaries in Nairobi are generally paid "at the end of the month," although now some people are paid on the fifteenth and thirtieth. In order to take advantage of this situation, the social hall committee decided that men would pay 1 shilling for admission to the hall from the thirtieth of the month to the sixth of the next month and on the fifteenth and sixteenth, while the fee would be half a shilling from the seventh to the fourteenth and from the seventeeth to the twenty-ninth. Women always paid half a shilling.

While the volume of business in the hall was high, the profit margin was not. One problem was that the village was unable to purchase bottled beer, soda, and cigarettes from a wholesaler who would give them sufficient credit or a good price. The result was that purchases were made on a daily basis, and the markup was only about 10 per cent. There was also the problem of "free beers." Government officials, police officers, and KANU functionaries visited the community regularly and expected the village leader to provide them with free beer and food. Although there were no records kept, it is clear that a good deal was consumed every month in this fashion.

Management of the hall was a complicated matter because of the high volume of business comprising a large number of very small transactions. In addition, the dances in the hall had been held on a regular basis for only several months when I first arrived in the community, which meant that the leaders were still in the process of developing regular rules which would govern its use. The minutes of the village committee and social hall committee meetings reflect this process of rule-making in the early months.

Many of the early questions revolved around the problem of selling locally brewed beer in the hall. First the committee decided to charge ten shillings to nonmembers and four shillings to members each time they sold their beer in the hall. However, the committee would permit only one person to sell beer at a time, and the demand was high. This was because selling beer in the hall provided a large market, which meant that the beer would be sold quickly, and it was very safe because of an informal agreement that the police had with the village leaders not to raid the hall and arrest people inside on charges of beer brewing, selling, or possession. The committee first decided to limit the number of times any person could sell beer in the hall, and favored applications from people who had not had a chance to do so. Later, they moved to allow only members to sell their beer in the hall, and subsequently they decided that each person selling beer in the hall could sell only one drum at a time. The success of beer selling in the hall led the committee to further limit selling by individuals; they first decided that the hall would brew and sell its own beer on the first and sixteenth of each month, and later they decided that the hall would brew and sell beer itself all the time.

Another problem that was brought up continually in the meetings was that of organizing and paying the people who worked in the hall on a regular basis. The committee sought to standardize rules of behavior and salaries for the workers and to define certain special jobs. Specific individuals were placed in charge of the generator, ticket collecting, and taking the inventory every morning. The committee also decided that the people working in the hall would receive 1/75 shillings per day for food. Other individuals are paid one to two shillings a day for specific tasks such as repairing the hall or cleaning the latrines.

The hall became extremely important to the village as a center of activity, as an important source of revenue, because of its role as an employer, and as a symbol of community achievement. One of the reasons that people in the village supported the hall and other community institutions was that in the long run they hoped to be able to obtain land. A more immediate goal was to use village funds for the immediate improvement of living conditions in Mathare Valley. Thus the village leaders usually had strong support for most community projects, including the nursery school and the water project.

The nursery school

During the election campaign in 1963 the KANU Mathare branch built a stone building to serve as party headquarters in an open area along Juja Road between villages 2 and 3. After the election, the M.P. for the area, Dr. Munyua Waiyaki, suggested that the building be turned into a KANU nursery school for children from Mathare Valley. By 1967 about 150 children between the ages of four and eight attended daily, and the villages paid a small salary to several teachers.

In October, 1967, Kiboro got permission from the district officer to add an extension to the social hall, and another classroom, which accommodated about forty additional students every day, was added in Village 2. The building was constructed in three or four days at a cost of about 600 shillings, about half of which went for wood and nails, with the balance being used to purchase aluminum sheets for the roof. Labor for the building was supplied by villagers. Men did most of the skilled work—the carpentry and measuring—while women did the actual construction of the mud walls. While visiting the construction site, I observed between twenty and sixty people working on the building at various times.

The nursery school is a place where parents can send their children if they cannot afford the fees in city schools. Children in the school begin to learn to read and write in Swahili. In addition, children who complete one or two years in the school can gain admission to government schools and receive credit for their time. During my visit, Kiboro became relatively successful at gaining school fee remissions (scholarships) for students from the nursery school who transferred to city schools, and spent a great deal of time at the beginning of the school year visiting headmasters and making applications on behalf of the mothers.

The water supply

One of the most common problems in squatter communities throughout the world is the provision of basic health and sanitation services, such as garbage collection, regulation of latrines or toilets, and a clean water supply. As long as a community remains relatively small or spread out, the first two problems are usually left to individuals to work out for themselves. As communities become larger and more densely settled, communities often find it necessary to lay down simple rules. In Mathare, the village committee appointed several "health inspectors" whose duty was to patrol the village and get people to clean up the area around their houses. In addition, the leaders tried to make sure that latrines were not built too close to the houses and were a certain minimum size.

Developing and enforcing such rules and regulations is not very expensive, as the community relies on local individuals. In contrast, the provision of clean water is a problem whose solution is often quite expensive. In Mathare Village 2, two supplies of clean water existed since the early 1960s. The first, located in the center of the village near the social hall, is a spring that was tapped to supply clean, filtered water. At certain times of the year, however, the flow is very weak and not nearly adequate for the needs of the several thousand people living in the village. A second source is water which is collected by young men from a gas station or from shops in nearby Eastleigh and sold to villagers in four-gallon tins. The problem with this source of water is its high cost.

Therefore, about a year before this study began, the village leaders requested the city government of Nairobi to sell clean water to the village from the city's supply, with the villagers purchasing the necessary pipes and a water meter. The response was that the city was unable to sell the water because as squatters the people in the village had no legal standing. Nevertheless, the leaders went ahead with the project, installed the pipes, bought a water meter, and started to pay an Asian building contractor for water which was taken from his supply. This arrangement did not work out very well, as there were arguments about the cost of the water and about several minor details; finally the community arranged to purchase water from the Catholic church in the area. The new supply flows much faster than the spring water, but is not free, as villagers pay a tenth of a shilling per four-gallon can.

The installation of the water supply was an expensive investment for the community, despite the fact that local labor was used whenever possible. The pipes had to be purchased and a plumber had to be hired to do some of the specialized work. Then, during my stay, the community had to raise money to purchase the water meter and to pay the deposit. Early in December, 1967, Kiboro called a public meeting in the village and announced that the district commissioner had given the village committee permission to collect money for the water project for a limited amount of time, and that the committee had decided to tax everyone owning a room in the village eleven shillings. Several weeks later he held another public meeting, during which he talked more or less nonstop for three or four hours, asking people to pay their eleven shillings and discussing various community problems. At the end of three weeks, the village had received the eleven shillings from 220 people, which meant that over three-quarters of the people owning at least one room had paid the tax. This figure is extraordinarily high considering that the payment was voluntary; the village committee has no official taxing power and the district commissioner had only authorized the leaders to collect the money, but did not in any way compel payment. In addition, government authorities in Nairobi contend that Mathare is one of the centers of tax evasion in the city, and hundreds of people are usually arrested for nonpayment when police come to the village and ask to see tax receipts.

KANU Mathare

Because the village chairman is also the vice-chairman of the Nairobi Northwest constituency, he is active in local politics, and it is difficult to separate his party role from his role as village chairman or head of the cooperative society. He is able to provide the party with supporters for political rallies and with voters on election day. Despite the large number of substantive demands that he makes to government officials in private, he makes a point of praising the government and its leaders at all public meetings. Furthermore, his party role has introduced him to many people in the city who have helped him strengthen his leadership position in the village.

Party membership cards are sold in the village, although hardly anyone bought one during the time I was there. In general, although people from the village would occasionally go to rallies or KANU meetings throughout the Nairobi area, relatively little overt party activity took place in the village.

The savings and credit cooperative

In 1966 the village leaders formed a savings and credit cooperative which sold shares to members in the same way that the social hall did. Each share cost twenty shillings, and any member could buy up to ten shares. In October, 1967, there were 94 members who had bought a total of 308 shares, giving the society an income of over 6,000 shillings. Members of the cooperative could obtain small loans, but relatively few did so, and the bank balance was usually several thousand shillings. The cooperative was important to the leaders because it provided a mechanism for accumulating capital in the community, thus enabling the village to purchase land if an opportunity presented itself. Just before my arrival, in fact, they made a down payment on some land, but the purchase was not approved by the government. The cooperative society was not especially active, although it did hold meetings every few months.

The KANU youth wing

The youth wing of the political party is the police force of the community. It consists of about ten people who are supported by a one-shilling assessment that is collected from residents once a month, and who occupy rooms given to them by the village committee. The youth wing members pass through the village and are charged with breaking up fights and generally keeping order. If a situation gets too rough (for example, if two men are fighting with knives or *pangas*), the youth wing may take them to the police. As with other law-enforcement groups, the occasional abuse of his position on the part of a youth wing member is one of the major problems for the village committee. Some members have been dismissed and ordered to return their uniforms and leave their rooms, but in many cases little action is taken.

Dispute settlement

The village elders sit as a group to hear disputes that arise in Mathare 2. Kariuki Gichohi, the village vice-chairman, is officially in charge of the elders, who have no regularly scheduled meetings but get together as cases arise. The elders, like the other community institutions, have no legal standing in the eyes of the wider society. Their authority to hear cases and impose decisions depends totally upon the willingness of the parties involved in a case to present it to the group and to abide by the decision.

A large proportion of cases reported to the elders either are never heard or are referred to another body, such as the government courts or police, for action. In about half the cases, the elders listen to the different parties and offer a judgement. Their presence in the community and the kinds of decisions they make are important integrative forces in the village.

An analysis of 200 cases recorded in Mathare 2 from November, 1966, to January, 1968, revealed a range of content areas in cases presented to the elders as shown in Table 6.1. The most frequent cause of disputes, accounting for about a quarter of all cases, involves fighting, general arguments, and insults or name calling. Vying for position as the second most important category are the collection of debts, such as rents, and quarrels between members of a household or disputes over sexual rights. Next were cases concerned with property theft and then cases involving rights to property, such as a business, a room, or clothing. Finally, there were disputes involving village business, and those concerned with traditional rituals or witchcraft.

TABLE 6.1 CONTENT AREA OF CASES REPORTED TO MATHARE ELDERS, BY DEGREE OF RESOLUTION

	Fighting	Debt Collection	Household Disputes	Theft	Right to Property	Village Business	Witch-craft	Total
Reported	44%	37%	28%	37%	19%	18%	30%	34%
Heard, but not resolved	10	0	16	26	4	0	20	11
Resolved	46	63	56	37	77	82	50	55
	100%	100%	100%	100%	100%	100%	100%	100%
Number of cases	59	32	32	30	26	11	10	200

Cases are brought to the elders through several channels. Some individuals come to the social hall and ask for a hearing of their complaint. A short version of the case, giving only the barest of details, is put in writing, and the individual is told that the elders will let him know when the case can be heard. Kariuki, if he is not in the office at the time, is notified, and he begins to make arrangements for a meeting. A second channel for reporting cases is the village youth wing, which often reports disputes to the village leaders. In some situations, such as fights, the youth wing might even bring one or both of the parties to the social hall so that the dispute can be heard immediately. The third channel for bringing cases is referral from one of the village leaders, who will suggest to an individual that he file a complaint with the elders.

Cases reported but not heard

About a third of the cases (68 of the 200 discussed above) never get beyond the stage of being reported. In some cases this is because the second party to a dispute refuses to appear before the elders, as in the following:

> Two Luo women were partners in brewing beer. One time when they made and sold beer one of the women kept all the money and then made her own batch of beer the next time. The other woman went to the elders and said she wanted to know where the profits were, but the first woman refused to appear before the elders.

Sometimes neither party will return to have the case heard.

> One man loaned 100 shillings to a woman and then she refused to repay it. He came to the elders and asked them to help him collect the debt. He does not live in the village and has never shown up again.

> Two ladies from the village were fighting and were told by the elders to return for the hearing of the case. They never did.

A third reason why cases do not progress beyond this stage is that it is often impossible to find the second party in a case.

> A man and his brother returned to the village late at night and went to sleep in the man's room, where there was also a third man sleeping. When the man awoke in the morning his money and clothing (totaling 350 shillings) were gone, as was the third man.

> A woman said she was walking with another girl from a shop at about 7:30 one evening. The girl saw two men approaching them and ran ahead, but the first woman continued to walk slowly as usual. The woman said she was caught and they hit her on the face with a club. As she fell, they started to run away. She saw another man in front of her and cried for help, but he didn't come. Finally she got up slowly and walked to a friend's house. Someone went to get her sister, who came with an old man; he called her brother, who notified the police. She said she didn't know who beat her, but would ask the elders to hear the case if she ever saw him again.

A last reason why some cases are never heard is that their being reported may convince the parties to resolve the dispute before a hearing is held.

> A man was loaned 150 shillings by another man when he was building a house, and after the completion of the house he refused to pay the money back. The man who made the loan reported the case to the elders and then the second man repaid the money before the elders had a chance to hear the case.

> A man sent his wife to the rural areas and then began to live with another woman. When the wife returned she saw that the blankets were dirty and bloody. He told her to wash them but she said she couldn't because she didn't know whose blood it was. He beat her and then she brought the case to the elders. The husband was summoned to appear, but he quickly made amends to his wife so the case was never heard.

The probability that a case will be heard after it is reported depends on its content. Cases involving fighting, debt collection, or theft are least likely to move beyond the reporting stage, in contrast with those involving questions of property rights or village business. In fighting or theft cases it is often particularly difficult to locate the second party, while in debt collection cases there may be an outright refusal to appear before the elders, as they have no power to compel appearance. Thus, in about two out of every five cases in these areas a complaint is filed, but no additional action is taken, as is shown in Table 6.1.

Cases heard but not resolved

A second category of decisions, accounting for 11 per cent of the cases, involves situations where the elders hold a hearing but are apparently unable to offer an opinion. Often they cannot reach a decision because they have no way of determining which of the two parties is relating the facts correctly. Realizing the dilemma, they may either drop the case entirely at this point, citing the contradictions, or they may suggest that either or both of the parties take the case to the government courts or to the police.

> A man from Meru went to a woman with 165 shillings. He said he counted the money in front of her. They slept together and the following morning he found 80 shillings missing. When he accused the woman of stealing she denied it. She also told the elders that he had never counted the money in front of her. The case was dropped as there were no witnesses.

The elders are aware of the limits of their ability to make decisions; they maintain their legitimacy by rejecting cases they consider outside their capabilities. In a number of cases they explicitly suggest that the dispute be taken elsewhere for final resolution. Often the recommended authority is the government courts or the police, but sometimes a traditional means of solution may be advised, such as consulting the father of a woman if there is a dispute as to where she should live.

> A woman ran away from her husband in Limuru and came to Mathare. He came to the village, but didn't want to take her back. He just sought the name of the man she was living with. The husband had previously filed a case in Limuru seeking the return of the brideprice he had paid (3,350 shillings) and of money (70 shillings) she had taken to her parents. The court had refused to grant him the award and told him they should stay together. The woman's parents also came to Mathare. The elders called for the woman, handed her to her parents, and said that the husband should file another case in the courts.

> A man sought a divorce from his wife, saying he wanted to live alone. He said he would accept any decision of the elders. They ruled that they had no right to grant the divorce and that the man would have to ask his wife's father for it. The woman then returned to her father and decided to bring a case against the husband.

> A man came to the village to deliver milk to some shops. When he returned to his truck he found that someone had stolen some milk and refused to pay. Rather than handle the case, the elders said the matter should be brought to the police since a businessman and someone from outside the village were involved.

Resolved cases

In the remaining 55 per cent of the cases, some sort of resolution is reached by the elders. In some situations nothing more is required than that the elders hear the facts in a case, for there is actually nothing for them to decide.

> A Kisii man said he didn't want to live with his wife any more. He sent his wife and children away and called the elders as witnesses, and said that if she came back he would take the case to Court.

In most cases, however, the elders need to make some determination as to the relevant facts in the case, and in doing this they will continue only if the major parties are in basic agreement, unless there are witnesses that will clearly support one of the positions. In some situations this process is straightforward, and a decision is reached without great difficulty.

> A man gave a friend of his a coat to wear. The friend in turn gave it to a third man. The man who owned the coat complained to the elders. The second man admitted that he had done this and the elders ruled he would have to pay 30 shillings, the value of the coat. Both agreed to accept the decision.

> A woman purchased a dress for 10 shillings and a balance of 7 shillings remained. She was called before the elders and ordered to pay the balance before them, which she did.

Other cases are quite complicated, and a large number of facts need to be straightened out before a decision can be reached.

> A woman from the village had her sweater stolen. One day she was in Village 3 and saw another woman wearing it. She approached the woman and demanded to know where the sweater came from. The woman replied that a certain youth wing member from Village 2 had given it to her one night when he brought her into his house through the window. He said he bought it for her because he loved her. The next morning he didn't let her leave and finally at noon when he left, locking the door behind him, she jumped out the window. The youth wing member told the elders he got the sweater from the canteen. "From whom?" he was asked. No one. He said he took it because he felt cold. He admitted knowing the woman from Village 3, but he said he didn't say to her that he bought the sweater. He had told her that if she would come with him he had a friend who would pay to sleep with her. He gave her three shillings and then demanded that she pay him 1 shilling as rent for the bed (which was actually public property because it was in the youth wing house). He admitted this. The elders asked the woman whose sweater it was what she wanted. She said another sweater

worth 5 shillings. The elders saw that the sweater was worth more and they said it should be 15 shillings. They ruled that the youth wing member should not enter the canteen because of his actions and ordered him to pay 15 shillings for the sweater. He was also rebuked for charging rent for public property—the 1 shilling bed rent.

A young woman came to Mathare and soon after a young man came along and became involved with her. For a while they were living together, but finally they had a fight and she left him. The man went to the elders and said he wanted his wife back, claiming he had paid the full brideprice. She disagreed and said it had not been paid. Unable to resolve the problem, the elders sent the couple to the rural areas with several youth wing members; the father wrote back that the brideprice was not yet paid. Therefore, the elders concluded that the woman had a right not to live with the man.

Listening to witnesses or visiting individuals concerned, as in the above case, is one way in which the elders attempt to determine the facts in a particular case. Another mechanism is reliance on traditional witch doctors. The two parties visit the witch doctor and the accused is told to eat a piece of bread. Inability to swallow it reveals guilt.

A lady left some money in a pillow case. 100 shillings was stolen and she accused another woman and said they should go together to the witch doctor. The other woman was unable to swallow the bread. When they returned she gave the first woman 40 shillings and left a watch with the elders as deposit for the remaining 60 shillings.

In seeking to resolve a dispute, the elders work toward a restitutive rather than a punitive solution. As in urban courts in other parts of Africa (Epstein 1958:chap. 6), there is more emphasis on determining what injustice has occurred and then correcting it than on punishing the guilty party. A person who has not paid a debt or an individual found guilty of theft is told to remit the money or return the property in question to the rightful owner. However, there is no additional punishment for the guilty party. Similarly, two people brought before the elders for fighting are often told that people in the village need to get along, and that they shouldn't fight any longer. In reaching a decision, the elders consider not only the wrong that needs to be corrected, but also the capabilities of the two parties for achieving a just solution. In one case reported to the elders, a shopkeeper asked for assistance in collecting a debt of Shs. 227/95 from an old man in the community who had bought goods on credit. The elders called the man, but he never appeared. They dropped the matter because they knew how poor he was and that he would never be able to pay the debt anyway. A similar problem is involved in the following case:

> A man wanted 200 shillings plus interest returned to him from a woman to whom he had loaned the money nine months before. He wanted 540 shillings all together. The elders heard the case and agreed, but pointed out that since the woman was poor she would have to pay back the money slowly. They set a limit of 30 shillings a month, which she is paying now.

The only decisions to which this generalization does not apply are those which concern village business, such as the running of the social hall. In such cases a person may be either warned not to misbehave in the future or dismissed from his work with the social hall or the youth wing.

> A member of the social hall staff entered and found people drinking. He banged a table and knocked over people's drinks. The same day he started to sell tickets and pocketed the money after the dance was over. He was taken off his job in the hall, but allowed to stay with the youth wing.

Thus, in dealing with local institutions where villagers have made the rules and where they have the capacity for enforcement, the elders' decisions are often punitive.

Enforcement of legal decisions

For the most part the elders are unable to enforce their decisions. Except for cases such as the one cited above, concerning the man working in the social hall, compliance rests with the two parties in the dispute. In some cases there is no explicit action required from either party—for example, when they are warned by the elders not to continue fighting. In most situations, however, one of the parties must either pay money to the other, return property, or recognize the other's right to action or property.

From the data available on each case, it is not possible to know what percentage of the elders' decisions were actually carried out. In only one or two cases did a party return to the elders because the other had refused to comply with the decision. There are, however, some cases in which both individuals may be unwilling or unable to abide by the decision.

A man of 28 had been away from his wife for about three years. His family from Nyeri and hers from Kiambu sat together at a meeting with the elders. They all decided that the couple should separate, and their belongings were divided. The two people did not really want to do this, but the families and the elders were quite insistent, so they swore before the elders they would stay apart although the elders could not prevent them from returning to Mathare. Subsequently both returned to the village and have come back together, but they are ashamed to bring the matter back to the elders.

At other times there are individuals who just do not comply with a decision, even when they accept it.

A man rented a bar. The man who had previously rented it left a pot there. One day he sent his son to collect it, and found out that the man working for the new owner had sold it. He went to the elders seeking compensation. They said he should be paid for the pot and the new owner agreed, but has yet to pay the money.

Dispute settlement and community integration

The elders in Mathare 2 are particularly important in achieving the peaceful resolution of disputes, which is one of the key marks of a politically integrated community. Although they are unable to handle all disputes effectively, and despite the fact that they have no power to enforce their decisions, the range and number of cases brought to the elders indicate their importance to community members. In addition, the elders direct the interest and attention of people in Mathare to a local institution, emphasizing the importance of the community.

The elders provide a widely accepted mechanism for settling individual differences in a manner which permits both sides to maintain respect. The decision-making of Mathare elders seems to have many parallels with dispute settlement by clan elders in traditional Kikuyu society (Lambert 1956; Middleton and Kershaw 1953). Two important differences are the absence of a kinship basis for the selection of Mathare elders and their inability to enforce their decisions. The first difference reflects the influence of urban migration and settlement patterns, while the second was also a problem in certain traditional situations.

An example of the role of the elders is shown in cases where a landloard wishes to evict a tenant for nonpayment of rent or for any other reason. The village committee passed a rule that there could be no eviction without the consent of the elders. Therefore, a number of cases are presented in which a landlord explains why he wishes to evict a particular renter. In a good number of cases, it is simply because rents are past due, and the elders are able to impress the importance of payment upon the renter and to get the two parties to agree to a schedule of payments. Their intervention in the matter prevents an ugly personal conflict from occurring in the community and, in addition, provides a mechanism for conflict resolution that is equally respected by both sides.

Measures of Mathare's integration

The presence and activity of community-wide political structures in Mathare 2 are the clearest indicators of political integration in the community. From the above description of their operation, we can develop indicators of the sense of community and the strength of institutions, the two components of political integration. It is useful to develop multiple measures for these two, or any other, variables in attempting to measure as broad a concept as political integration. If in fact the scores on a number of different measures are highly interrelated, then one has greater assurance that the concept is being adequately evaluated. At the same time, if the scores on one or two of the measures are widely divergent from the scores on other indicators, then the researcher must ask whether his concept is multidimensional or whether his measures are inadequate. In some cases evidence from one measure may be ignored as convergence on a larger number of measures increases the researcher's confidence in his findings. A second way to evaluate the confidence with which particular findings should be accepted is to evaluate the over-all adequacy of the indicators themselves (Naroll 1962).

Our particular problem is to construct measures of sense of community and institutional strength appropriate to Mathare 2. Table 6.2 presents eleven indicators of political integration—five measuring sense of community and seven indicating institutional strength—along with an assessment of the quality or adequacy of each indicator and the score of the community on each measure. The quality of the indicator is an assessment of the extent to which the proposed indicator adequately measures the concept it is intended to measure; the score, which can range from very high to very low, suggests the value of

TABLE 6.2 MEASURES OF POLITICAL INTEGRATION IN MATHARE 2

Concept		Indicator	Quality of Indicator	Score in Mathare 2
Sense of community	1.	Researcher's impression of the extent to which residents perceived themselves to be members of a distinct political community	Fair	High
	2.	Researcher's impression of the strength of positive identification with Mathare 2	Fair	Medium
	3.	Voluntary payment of assessments for the youth wing and village projects such as water project	Good, indirect measure	Medium High
	4.	Voluntary work on village projects, such as the nursery school or water project	Fair, indirect measure	Medium
	5.	Survey questions determining degree of identification with the community	Excellent, but not available	?
Strength of institutions	1.	Range of tasks undertaken by community institutions	Excellent	Very High
	2.	Size of budget of community institutions	Good	High/ Very High
	3.	Number of people working in one or more of the community institutions	Good	High/ Very High
	4.	Extent to which community institutions make binding decisions	Good	Low/ Medium
	5.	Extent of compliance with and/or implementation of decisions	Good	Medium

TABLE 6.2 CONTINUED

Concept		Indicator	Quality of Indicator	Score in Mathare 2
	6.	Researcher's impression of the ability of institutions to manage substantive problems effectively	Good	High
	7.	Survey questions determining the degree to which people are satisfied with the way in which institutions handle community problems	Excellent, but not available	?

that measure in Mathare 2. The score represents a combination of two elements: the potential for increase or decrease in this measure within Mathare 2, and a comparison of the score for Mathare 2 on this variable with other communities and neighborhoods in Nairobi, particularly other squatter villages in the Mathare area. Included in the list of measures are two for which no data are available. These both represent potentially excellent measures of integration in Mathare and are listed as a possible means of evaluating the adequacy of the measures which are actually used.

Sense of community

The first two measures of sense of community involve the researcher's impressions, on the basis of participant observation in the community, of: (1) the extent to which residents perceive themselves to be members of a distinct political community; and (2) the strength of positive identification with this distinct community. While there was certainly a range of variation within Mathare 2 on both of these measures, the score on each represents a composite or average which tries to take this variation into account. The first measure, the perception of Mathare as a distinct political community, is scored slightly higher than the second, the strength of positive identification with the community. One possible explanation of this scoring is that many residents identify with other social groups, such as their families, their tribe, and in some cases even the nation of Kenya, as well as with Mathare. Thus, recognition of the distinctiveness of Mathare 2 and of the position of urban squatters does not necessarily lead to the development of a positive identification with this distinct community.

The two remaining indicators of sense of community are indirect in that they are based on inferences from behavior rather than on direct assessments of the attitude itself: (3) voluntary payment of assessments for the youth wing and village projects, such as the water project; and (4) voluntary work on village projects, such as the construction of the nursery school or the water project. In discussing possible measures of attitudinal integration, Nye suggests that such behavioral indicators can be important as a check on "cost-free verbal statements" in indicating sacrifice or trust in a community (1971:47). The voluntary contribution of money or labor in Mathare indicates a commitment to the community, as members who contributed used their own resources to serve community needs. Payment of money for the completion of the water project was a particularly dramatic indicator, as three-quarters of those asked to contribute eleven shillings did so. In a country where tax collection rates are low, and in a community where evasion of government taxes is widespread, this figure is truly astounding. At the same time, the monthly payment of one shilling for the youth wing from each household usually shows 50 to 75 per cent nonpayment.[1] Contributions of labor to village projects were harder to assess, as some jobs, such as part of the water project, required particular skills which not everyone possessed; other jobs, such as the nursery school construction, took place in a small space where

1. This is a very sketchy impression; I have no adequate data on this question.

only a limited number of people could work. Nonetheless, it appears that the donation of labor in village projects was lower than the payment of village assessments, and thus its score is slightly lower. At the same time, it should be noted that there is no evidence of either of these practices—the donation of money or the volunteering of labor for communal needs—in any neighborhoods of the city outside of the Mathare area.[2] Mathare 2 was probably more effective in money raising than the other mathare villages, but not much different in terms of its ability to get people to work on community projects.

Strength of institutions

The operation of Mathare 2's community-wide institutions was extensively observed, and therefore good measures were more easily developed for institutional strength than for sense of community. The first three measures directly assess the activity of community institutions: (1) the range of tasks undertaken by community institutions; (2) the size of the budget of community institutions (relative to the total wealth of the community); and (3) the number of people working in one or more of the institutions (i.e., the bureaucracy). Each of these seeks to evaluate the significance of the community-wide activities in Mathare 2 in a slightly different way. The range of tasks handled by various Mathare institutions is possibly the best indicator of their strength. Even two problems which are the most pressing concerns of Mathare residents, jobs and permanent land tenure, were issues that the community sought to deal with directly, although it could not be considered to have been fully successful in either. The community does provide jobs, such as those in the social hall or youth wing, but these are far fewer than the number needed. The community's budget is quite high, particu-

2. Two exceptions are the Langata squatter community in the western part of the city and the Kibera settlement, still predominantly Somali, also in western Nairobi.

larly in light of the fact that payment of assessments is voluntary and not legally sanctioned. One factor contributing to the size of the budget is the operation of the social hall, which, while it did not make a good profit, did circulate money in the community and provide funds for emergencies, such as large-scale arrests or hospitalization. The hall is also responsible for most of the jobs generated in the community, giving people subsistence wages in return for work done in and around the hall. Counting these people as well as the village leaders and youth wing members, a rough count showed that between fifty and seventy-five people or about 5 to 8 per cent of the adult population, worked in the village institutions.

The next two measures of institutional strength deal directly with the question of authority and its exercise in Mathare 2: (4) the extent to which community institutions made decisions which were binding; and (5) the extent to which decisions were complied with and implemented. According to both of these measures, as is seen in Table 6.2, the institutions' scores were weaker than they were on the measures of organizational activity. The status of decisions reached in Mathare is that most are neither clearly legal nor clearly illegal. Often the government sanctions and legitimizes the authority of the village leaders (a point which will be discussed at greater length in chapter 8) and, as in the case of the water project, specifically authorizes the collection of funds. At the same time, decisions can be ignored within the community if a person chooses to do so, although in some situations he may risk public criticism or social ostracism.[3] Most important, decisions reached in the community cannot be enforced outside the community, and cases in which decisions are reached by the elders and implemented usually

3. It is interesting that one of the community groups that Kiboro often chided for noncompliance with his authority was the small shopkeepers. As is discussed below, they are relatively independent economically and less subject to outside threat and police action than are the people whose economic subsistence depends upon beer brewing.

involve two parties from Mathare. Compliance with decisions is generally high, however, as people recognize the legitimate character of the decisions themselves. Thus, people involved in a case will often appear voluntarily before the elders even if they know that the decision will go against them. Furthermore, people generally respect village regulations and decisions, partially because they do not want to incur the wrath of the village leaders and partially because they realize their potential dependence on the leaders in any future crisis.

The final measure of institutional strength is the over-all effectiveness of the community institutions in dealing with problems arising in Mathare 2. An ideal measure of this would be obtained through survey research, aimed at getting people to rate their satisfaction with the workings of the institutions and with institutional leaders. Since survey data are unavailable, effectiveness was measured by: (6) the researcher's impression of the ability of institutions to manage substantive problems effectively. The high score on this measure is due to the fact that most people appeared to perceive the handling of problems as being as effective as possible, even though in many cases successful resolution was never achieved. In unresolved cases, however, people's fatalism and feelings of powerlessness often emerged. Thus, rather than criticism of village leaders or institutions because conditions were not better, there was more often acceptance of the world as a place of inevitable difficulty and disappointment.

Conclusions

Mathare 2 has a relatively high level of political integration, and the measures presented in this section suggest that this is a result of a well-developed sense of community and of strong community institutions. At the same time, the analysis indicates that institutional strength is more important than sense of community in explaining the over-all high level of integration, as a composite index of each component might show sense of community to be medium/high and strength of institutions to be high. However, as these scores were simply crude ratings within one community, undue significance should not be attached to small differences.

Of greater importance is the task of attempting to explain why Mathare 2 has apparently achieved the high level of political integration outlined in this chapter. In seeking answers to this question, we begin with the hypotheses developed from the analysis of squatter communities throughout the world, and presented in chapter 4. At that time, we identified eleven variables which were important in explaining community cohesion and integration in other squatter areas. Now we can consider how adequately they explain the development of a sense of community and strong community institutions in Mathare 2.

7

Sense of community in Mathare 2

What are the conditions under which individuals living in an area develop a common sense of identity and a feeling that their needs and hopes are intertwined with those of others? In trying to answer this question in Mathare 2, we can begin with the variables identified in the review of squatter communities in developing countries. The strength of feelings that make up a sense of community are hypothesized to be a function of: (1) the perceived importance of the community in the lives of participants; (2) the level of threat to participation and membership in the community; (3) the existence of highly affective symbols particularly associated with the community; and (4) the level of participation in specific political and social activities or rituals in the community.

Perceived importance of the community

There can be great variation in the extent to which people see their daily activities as linked to a single community. To what extent does an individual have a meaningful option concerning where he will live and how he will support himself and his family? We would expect that the fewer the choices open to him, and the more dependent he is on a particular community, the more important he perceives that community to be in his life, and the stronger the sense of community he feels. Urban neighborhoods are typically less important in the lives of their residents than rural communities. One explanation for this is the difference in isolation. A second is the degree of differentiation in the urban community, in which residence and economic activities are typically separated (Wirth 1938). Thus a person's livelihood is not necessarily tied economically to the community where he sleeps. The high degree of differentiation in urban areas is sometimes more theoretical than real, however. There are still many neighborhoods, even in the largest and most modern cities, where residents find their particular economic skills, as well as their emotional security, tied to specific communities.

In considering urban squatters, the question of the perceived importance of the community is linked to the question of alternatives. To what extent can the squatters live as well elsewhere? Two clear alternatives need to be evaluated—the rural and the urban. Wouldn't these people be better off if they went back to the land, as government bureaucrats and politicians often ask them to do? What about living in other parts of the city, in already established, legal neighborhoods? In Nairobi and Mathare 2, the answer to these two questions is relatively clear. The squatters lack both the rural alternatives, in the form of land holdings, and the urban skills needed to get permanent jobs in the city. As a result, their solution to the very real question of day-to-day survival is tied to the beer brewing, *pombe* economy which is highly location-specific in Mathare. Thus, in comparison with most urban dwellers in Nairobi and other cities, the residents of Mathare find themselves highly dependent on a single community, which is perceived as quite important in their lives. A more complete outline of the economics of survival in Mathare 2 will clarify this point.

The economy of Mathare 2

Mathare residents maintain relatively strong ties with their rural relatives, but this does not mean that they have meaningful rural alternatives. Over 80 per cent of the adults were born in Kiambu, Fort Hall, Nyeri, and Machakos districts, all of which are presently characterized by heavy population pressure and extremely small farms. Seventy-four per cent have no land holdings at all; and among those with some land, most of the farms are too small to provide a livelihood, even in the country-side. Only 14 per cent of the Mathare residents, for example, report that they have a farm of three acres or more in the rural areas, and only 1 per cent have more than six acres. For comparison, Table 7.1 presents data obtained in two other neighborhoods in Nairobi, Shauri Moyo and Kariokor, which suggests that the level of land holdings in Mathare 2 is considerably lower than it is for the urban population in general.[1]

TABLE 7.1 COMPARISON OF LAND OWNERSHIP OUTSIDE NAIROBI OF MATHARE RESIDENTS AND OTHER NAIROBI AFRICANS

| | SIZE OF FARM | |
	Mathare Residents	Nairobi Sample
Landless	74%	41%
3 acres or less	12	24
4-6 acres	13	15
More than 6 acres	1	20
	100%	100%
Sample size	233	496

1. For greater detail concerning the Shauri Moyo and Kariokor samples see Ross (1968:chap.4). The data from Mathare 2 come from interviews with 234 adults in the community. Of these, 219 were randomly selected from a list of all the rooms in the community which the village leaders had collected earlier, and 15 were village leaders selected because of their position in the community. The interviews were conducted in Swahili and Kikuyu between December, 1967, and February, 1968. Rempel (1972:27) presents data from a sample of migrants in Nairobi showing virtually the same distribution in land holdings as the Mathare sample, and far less than the Shauri Moyo and Kariokor people. However, he drew his sample only from migrants who came to Nairobi after independence in December, 1963, and we might expect these people to be different than the longer-term residents, particularly with respect to land holding. They are probably younger, less well established in the city, and less likely to have land of their own in the rural areas.

Urban employment opportunities are few and far between for Mathare 2 residents, given their level of skills and the job market in Nairobi. Since 1963 the number of people looking for work in the city has increased much more quickly than the number of jobs, and by 1970 a person with a degree from a secondary school would typically have a hard time finding work, as competition for jobs is fierce and the initial wave of Africanization in government has been completed. In Mathare, half the adults have never attended school at all, and only 3 per cent have gone beyond primary school, as opposed to 30 per cent for the Nairobi population in the other two neighborhoods (Shauri Moyo and Kariokor), as shown in Table 7.2. The figures are even more striking for Mathare women than for men, but for both sexes the differences between Mathare residents and Nairobi's wider population are considerable. The second part of Table 7.2 shows the occupational breakdown in Mathare 2, in comparison with the other parts of the city. While good data on employment are not easy to obtain, the overwhelming differences presented here show the concentration of the Mathare population among the unemployed and in low-paying jobs.

Thus people living in Mathare have little prospect of finding permanent jobs in the modern economic sector. Their response has been to subsist in the city by performing services no one else is interested in or able to perform and by taking a series of odd jobs that provide extremely low income. Instead of trying to compete with better-qualified individuals for the few existing jobs, most people in Mathare engage in one or more of the following money-making activities: beer brewing, prostitution, renting rooms, operating small shops, hawking fruits and vegetables, small-scale agricultural activities, part-time work, selling water, working in the village social hall, serving on the village committee or in the youth wing, and even petty theft. A short discussion of some of these activities shows their irregular character and the ways in which participation in several activities is often compatible.

TABLE 7.2 Comparison of Education and Occupation of Mathare Residents with Nairobi Africans, by Sex

	Education Level			
	Mathare Residents		Nairobi Sample	
	Male	Female	Male	Female
No school	42%	63%	13%	26%
Some primary school	33	29	26	30
Completed primary school	19	8	23	30
Beyond primary school	6	1	39	14
	100%	101%	101%	100%
Sample size	80	151	326	166

	Occupation			
	Mathare Residents		Nairobi Sample	
	Male	Female	Male	Female
Housewife	0%	5%	0%	38%
Clerical/sales employee	0	0	25	17
Small merchant/ artisan/self-employed	24	7	9	5
Professional/ business proprietor/ teacher/higher government official	3	1	13	8
Skilled worker	7	6	20	3
Manual/unskilled worker	23	14	22	14
Student	4	1	4	5
Farmer	1	0	0	3
Unemployed	37	65	7	7
	99%	99%	100%	100%
Sample size	70	144	312	162

Beer brewing

The brewing of beer is probably the most important single economic activity in the community. Fifty-six per cent of the residents report that they brew beer to sell at least once a month, while 43 per cent report that they brew beer regularly on the

TABLE 7.3 INCIDENCE OF BEER BREWING, BY SEX, AMONG MATHARE
RESIDENTS

	Male	Female	Total
Does not brew beer to sell	60%	37%	44%
About once a month	9	9	9
2-5 times per month	29	50	43
6 or more times per month	2	5	4
	100%	101%	100%
Sample size	81	153	234

weekends, as shown in Table 7.3 Despite the continual threat of arrest or police harassment because of its illegal nature, beer brewing represents the most regular and easiest way of earning money in Mathare. The profit, even considering the possibility of arrest and the cost of bribes, is decent, the work is not especially difficult, and the required capital is low.

Women are much more likely to engage in beer brewing and selling than men; at times, however, the activity is a common enterprise, with the men providing the capital and doing a portion of the heavy work while the women do most of the "cooking" and the selling. The women are usually paid a fixed amount of money for their labor. Arrangements vary widely, of course, depending not only on personal contacts but also on the kind and quantity of beer being made. It seems fair to say that for the most part beer selling, as opposed to its manufacture, is an activity most clearly identified with women in the community. This is due in part to their ability to attract customers, and in part it is related to the traditional role of Kikuyu and Kamba women, especially younger women, in serving men.

There are three different alcoholic drinks manufactured and sold in Mathare Valley. Most commonly found is *busa,* or millet beer, traditionally manufactured by the Luo, Baluhya, Kalenjin, and other tribes in western Kenya. In recent years it is also made and sold in municipal beer halls in many of the smaller Kenya towns. Its basic ingredients are maize meal, which has been cooked in an open pan over a hot fire, and millet. The process of fermentation in a large tin drum takes about eight days, after which the beer is strained and served. *Njohi*, or *mauratina*, a honey beer traditionally brewed among the Kikuyu and Kamba, is a second form of beer found in Mathare. This is made from sugar cane, honey, water, and a spongelike yeast. Total fermentation takes only a day or two. Finally, *shangaa*, or Nubian gin, a distilled alcohol, is found in the Mathare area. It is considered lethal if not properly made and is thought to cause blindness and death if consumed in excess. The leaders in Village 2 have prohibited its manufacture and sale in the community and I never saw or heard of it there, although it did exist in other villages in Mathare.

Millet beer is brewed most often because it can be made in large quantities and the profit is good. Generally an individual can expect a return of between 100 and 200 per cent in a very short period of time. Table 7.4 shows the costs involved in brewing a drum of millet beer for two men who bought the raw materials and then hired women to do almost all of the brewing and selling. They both pointed out that profits would have been higher if they had done all the work themselves and if no free samples had been given out. Unfortunately, however, they say that the usual practice is to give free samples so that people can taste before they buy.

TABLE 7.4 Costs Involved in Brewing and Selling Millet Beer in Mathare (in shillings)

	Credit	Debit
Cash received from sale	105/60	
Costs of materials		31/50
Costs of labor involved in brewing		15/—
Costs of labor involved in selling		10/—
Food for workers brewing beer		5/—
Total costs		61/50
Total profits		44/10

Prostitution

A second source of money for women in the village is payment for sexual favors, which takes a variety of forms. Some arrangements should be considered prostitution in only the strictest sense of the term. A women—often an older woman—may have a "regular" caller who visits once or twice a week, pays several shillings for a dinner and sexual rights, and possibly even acknowledges paternity of one or more of her children. This form of relationship has a much higher emotional content than other prostitute-client relationships.

In contrast, there are women who combine prostitution with their beer brewing and selling, offering their services to outsiders who are able to pay at least ten to twenty shillings. This sort of arrangement is much more strictly financial, although women often attempt to develop "regulars" from these casual contacts because of the prospect of steady income. Since these women are able to make contact with men through their beer trade, at the same time making known their sexual availability, the two activities complement each other.

A third form of prostitution, especially common among young women in their teens, might be termed "sexual experimentation." They become involved in sexual liaisons with young men from the village or Eastleigh, receiving only two or three shillings or a bottle of beer for their favors. Their primary interest is not really in making money, as is the case with more experienced prostitutes; on the other hand, they are aware that they can get something from young men by imitating the behavior of older women they know.

While prostitution exists in the village, its importance as an economic activity does not nearly equal that of beer brewing. A community such as Mathare does not attract people who can pay enough money to support many women in prostitution. In contrast to an area such as Eastleigh, where prostitution usually is not combined with beer brewing, in Mathare it is more commonly a supplemental money-making activity.

Renting rooms

A preferred source of income because of the low risk involved is renting rooms in the village. Unlike beer brewing and selling, there is no threat of arrest, and the only problems are nonpayment of rent and property damage caused by rainstorms or fire. Single rooms generally rent for between thirty and forty shillings a month. Thus a person owning four rooms who lives in one and rents out the other three can earn about a hundred shillings a month, provided his tenants pay regularly.

Ownership of rooms in the village is widely dispersed, however, and therefore few people are able to live solely on their income from rentals. According to the records of the village committee, in 1967 there were 674 rooms in the village owned by 277 different people—an average of about 2.4 rooms per owner. Furthermore, according to their figures, 61 individuals owned four or more rooms. The interviews with the residents also showed a wide dispersion of ownership, with 71 per cent of the population reporting that they owned at least one room. Of these owners, over half held only one room each. Only 11 per cent of the total population held four or more rooms, 24 per cent owned two or three rooms, and 36 per cent owned one room.

Room ownership is important not only because it is a possible source of income, but also because it removes the necessity of paying a monthly rent. People who own rooms in the village either were among the early arrivals who built their own homes, or they have bought one or more rooms from someone else. There are occasionally new rooms built today, but building is strictly limited by the government, which has agreed to permit existing houses to stand, but which regularly destroys new ones. The fact that no new houses can be built, combined with the housing squeeze in Nairobi, has driven up prices of rooms which are sold and, to some extent, has caused an increase in rents. The anticipated destruction of Pumwani, for example, sharply increased demand for rooms in Mathare in 1967 and 1968, so that single rooms often were sold for as much as five hundred to seven hundred shillings, although they cost less than a quarter of this to build.

Room rental is a favored economic activity not only because of its low risk, but also because of its quick return on a relatively small investment. The houses in the village are constructed of traditional materials, and the only costs to the builder are the wooden poles that are used for the frame, cartons (or, rarely, sheet metal) for the roof, and the wages paid to several women and children for mudding the walls, and possibly to a carpenter for helping to build the frame. An average four-room house in the village with a carton roof costs several hundred shillings to build. If the owner lives in one of the rooms and rents out the other three, the total cost should be returned within six months, after which time all the rental income represents profit on the investment.

Small shops and petty trade

About sixty to eighty people operate small *dukas*, or shops, in the village on a regular basis. A number of others trade in the open air or are hawkers less regularly. Most of the shops are located on the main street of the village, and sell primarily to the villagers. None is very large or well stocked, although some are clearly more prosperous and better run than others, and a few even have employees. Most common are general provision stores which sell packaged goods such as maize meal, sugar, salt, dried beans, soda, matches, and cigarettes. In addition there are several bars which sell bottled beer and soda, *hotelis* (small restaurants) which serve tea throughout the day and cooked meals at noon and in the evening, butchers who sell roasted as well as uncooked meat, a barber shop, and a large and prosperous carpentry shop.

Some of the businesses receive regular deliveries from wholesalers, while others are very poorly stocked and are often open at irregular hours. Many of the businesses are run by people who decided, because they owned a room on the main street, that they would try to start a small shop. In some cases, their lack of experience made failure almost inevitable; they later rented the room to someone else and were content with the sixty or seventy shillings they could get for store rent.

It is very difficult to say what constitutes a business success or failure in a community such as Mathare. For one thing, individuals often have no alternative economic activity to engage in, other than beer brewing, which entails much more risk, Therefore, the rational economic choice is often to continue to operate a business which returns as little as 100 shillings or less in profit each month to its owner. Although he probably keeps the shop open eighty or ninety hours a week (which means that his income is about Shs. -/30 per hour), there is little else that he can do. Furthermore, since most shops trade in foods of one kind or another, he is always able to feed his family for less than it would cost if he had to buy the foods from another shop. There is always the chance, too, that he may make a success out of the business and find himself in a good financial position. Finally, running a shop is pleasant work. An owner is constantly in contact with people; he is handling money and managing his own affairs, which makes him feel important; and he is separated from other people in the village because of the high status associated with being a businessman in an independent Kenya.

Another form of business activity is open-air selling of vegetables and fruits and door-to-door hawking. Some people engage in this trade regularly, while others are only occasional traders. A few travel to nearby rural areas, such as Kiambu, or to one of the markets in the center of town to purchase vegetables, fruits, dried maize, or beans, which they then sell in the village at a higher price. While the profit is not large, their overhead is also very low. At most they have to pay for a bus ticket, although often they walk to the city markets. If they are able to sell products that they have grown themselves on small plots of land, the profit is much higher than if they had sold their produce in a rural market. While many of these small traders, like the owners of the small shops, get a very low return, it is higher than any alternative source of income other than beer brewing or prostitution (which they may also engage in from time to time).

Small-scale agricultural activities

The most economically valuable skills that most people in Mathare possess are their agricultural abilities. As pointed out above, 98 per cent were born in rural areas of Kenya, and most learned as children the rudimentary aspects of peasant agricultural practices throughout Central Province. They are not necessarily skilled in the most advanced techniques, but this is hardly necessary in planting the small plots to which they may have access. Each rainy season many people from the village plant a variety of staple crops—maize, beans, potatoes, cabbage, and tomatoes—which are either saved for consumption during the year or sold in the city.

The greatest barrier to practicing agriculture for Mathare residents is that they are generally landless. Most of those who own land or have access to land in the rural areas return during the rains to plant and harvest their crops. In addition, however, many people plant in open fields wherever they find them on the outskirts of Nairobi. The hillside opposite the village, on the other side of the Mathare River, for example, is always planted with maize and other crops. Women also use fields around the edges of Eastleigh and between Mathare and Kariobangi. Sometimes one person or several persons together may rent the rights to farm a small piece of land in Ngong or Kiambu when the owner is either unable or unwilling to plant in a particular season. The women will travel by bus, visiting the land at the beginning of the rains for planting, once or twice more to weed it, and then again at harvest time. In addition to planting crops, several people in the community raise and sell animals, usually chickens and goats. While the high density of the village prevents most people from keeping animals, they are found in some of the larger compounds at the edges of the village.

Part-time work

Many people in the village, particularly males, have specific skills that are sufficiently well developed to provide a source of income from time to time. Men who know some carpentry often earn money by helping people construct or repair their houses, or by making small pieces of furniture. Others are able to make a few shillings doing manual work in the area—carrying loads of wood from a truck or digging a ditch to help someone who is constructing a house. Employment of this sort is not only found in the village, but also occasionally obtained from one of the small shops or Asian contractors in Eastleigh. Teenage boys often make money by selling cans of clean water that they transport either from the water supply or from the gas station located at the top of the hill.

Working on community projects

About fifty people in the village are given a few shillings a day to "help them with food" for working in the social hall, with the youth wing, or on other community projects. Almost every night dances are held in the social hall. The musicians, the people who serve the beer, the ticket takers, the women who clean the hall, and the people who keep the books receive several shillings the next morning. This money is taken from the admission charges and the revenue from beer sales. The number of people receiving money each day is not always constant, often depending on the profits of the night before.

The youth wing is supported through a one-shilling tax levied each month against village residents, and with money earned by selling clean water. A few people also work in the community as "health inspectors," as teachers in the nursery school, and on other projects for which they receive a token payment. The amount of money paid to each person is quite small, but it permits them to subsist in the city.

The above discussion of the economic activities of Mathare residents illustrates several points. The first is that the people in the community have been able, through a variety of ways, to support themselves marginally in the center of a modern city, although they have almost no direct economic links to the urban economy. Those with full-time wage employment are in a distinct minority, and even among those with jobs, the vast majority work in the most menial and unskilled positions. Through a combination of legal, quasi-legal, and illegal activities, the people of Mathare Valley support themselves in an economy where there is almost no demand for additional people with their skills, and where there is no viable rural alternative to their urban subsistence. Second, the discussion points out that people in Mathare engage in a number of economic activities which provide a very low return because they have no other alternatives. People in the marginal sector of the urban economy accept the smallest of profit margins, as in their trading activities, or the highest of risks, as in beer brewing, in order to survive. Their total income through these activities is extremely low. More than 70 per cent report that their average income is less than 200 shillings a month—less than the minimum wage for government employees—while only 26 per cent of Shauri Moyo and Kariokor residents earn so little. At the opposite end of the spectrum, 4 per cent of the Mathare residents, as compared with 55 per cent of the other sample, earn more than 300 shillings. Twenty-four per cent of the Mathare residents and nineteen per cent of the Nairobi sample earn between 201 and 300 shillings a month.

The community is important in the lives of people in Mathare

2. They spend a great proportion of time there, and its location is tied to their economic survival. Their marginality limits their range of effective choices, and their dependence on their neighbors is seen most clearly in the cooperative efforts of the women engaged in beer brewing and selling, to be described below. In Turner's scheme, Mathare 2 falls somewhere between the two major types. Because of the location and growth of the community, it might be expected to have a higher proportion of employed people and nuclear family households. Mathare 2 is an incipient and improving community; however, the unavailability of employment in Nairobi and the lack of government services in the community provide an important upper limit to the level of improvement which is possible at present.

Threats to community participation and membership

Moderate levels of threat directed toward a group can help the group develop a common sense of identity. Outside threats can take several forms. The most limited form of threat is stigmatization and social ostracism directed at a group from the outside. While such stigmatization is not necessarily related to concrete actions against a group, it does signify the outsider's view that the members of the group share certain negative characteristics, and raises the potential for collective action at some later time. Thus, the greater the level of social ostracism from outside a community, the more likely that community members will develop a common identification (Becker 1963). In almost all cities where there are squatters, a common response from much of the wider urban population, and particularly from administrators and the elite, is the characterization of squatter settlements as unclean areas, dens of thieves, or hotbeds of radicalism. Squatters often develop a sense of unity in response to these outside characterizations. A second and more immediate threat to squatters is that of action by the government against the community, directed toward either regulating life in the community or, more important, moving against squatters because of their illegal status.

In Mathare 2 both forms of outside threat work to increase the sense of community in the area. While residents are aware of their general negative image in the wider urban society, they also believe there is little they can do to change it. The forms of threat they fear most are police intervention in the community in connection with illegal activities such as the beer brewing; government attempts to collect taxes; and, from time to time, the reminder that they are squatters living on land that is not theirs and that the government could force them to leave the area. One somewhat ironic reminder of this fact resulted from a 1969 incident in which a group of squatters managed to purchase a small plot of land in the Mathare area which was occupied at the time by other squatters. As soon as the purchase was completed, the purchasers took steps to try to have the residents removed.

The police threat to impose sanctions on illegal beer brewing activities is probably the most important outside threat in the daily lives of Mathare residents, as the police are also among the best customers in the village. A resident can legally brew beer only if he has been issued a permit by the "chief" (a government civil servant) in Pumwani. The chief grants permits to manufacture beer for ceremonial occasions, such as weddings, births, or circumcisions; however, possession of the permit does not authorize the sale of the beer. Police who frequently drink in the community and then take part in a raid on the village are especially dangerous, because they know who is likely to have beer in his room.

Specifically, the police pose three types of threats to beer brewers in the village: (1) the threat of arrest in a police raid authorized by the local police superintendent or another high-ranking officer; (2) the threat of arrest in a raid undertaken by several constables, possibly in retaliation against specific individuals; and (3) the threat of loss of profits because of policemen soliciting bribes. Each threat poses a slightly different type of problem and elicits a different reaction on the part of people in the village.

Police raids in Mathare take place more or less regularly, as the police do not permit the villagers to continually flaunt the established authority. In a raid, as many as sixty or seventy people may be arrested, and any beer found in the village may be poured on the ground. Often raids take place right before a holiday, when the police can expect to find large amounts of beer easily. The common response of villagers is to lock their rooms (with the beer inside) and walk away from their houses. If the police are persistent, however, or if they have reliable information, they will break into a room and spill the beer, often arresting anyone in the vicinity. Another police technique is to arrive just before dawn, when people are still sleeping and have no chance to leave their rooms. Although the police may release a few people who were arrested during such raids, most people are taken to court and forced to pay a fine, which usually ranges from thirty to fifty shillings, depending on the charge and the sentencing. These large-scale raids organized to produce results, the most concrete of which are arrests, are staged to demonstrate the efficiency of the police force to higher-ranking officials.

The threat of arrest also exists when one or more police constables decide to initiate a raid in the village, often in relatiation against specific individuals. For example, a policeman who has been refused a bribe or a free beer will often return with several friends when he is on duty. In another situation, a policeman involved in a fight may later arrest several people. After a raid of this sort, the police inspector has a greater range of options in dealing with the arrested people. Because he is under no pressure from headquarters in such situations, he is able to either lower the charge, accept a bribe and release the people arrested, or hold one or two people, releasing everyone else. His decision often depends on whether any of the arrested people know the inspector or whether any of the village leaders appear at the police station.

A third threat to beer brewers is presented by policemen solicting free drinks and bribes. In most cases, they ask for only a few free drinks, but at times they take advantage of their position by asking for twenty or thirty shillings and perhaps several bottles of European-style beer. When the demands are too steep, a villager may simply refuse to pay the bribe and instead accept arrest. In other situations, he may seek the assistance of a village leader in trying to either lower the bribe or get the policeman to leave. If the same policeman continues to harass villagers by soliciting excessive bribes for any length of time, the village leaders may first ask his superior officers to intervene; finally, they may appeal to political authorities. Police officials who recognize the village leaders and work with them usually respond favorably to their requests.

It is difficult to estimate the cost of police intervention in the village. During the period when the research was conducted, I estimated that at least fifty people a month were arrested on charges of illegally brewing, possessing, or selling beer. This does not include only villagers, as during raids police often arrest customers (sometimes off-duty policemen) as well. Since the average fine for those arrested and convicted is about 40 shillings, the fines alone cost at least 2,000 shillings per month.[2] The cost of bribes is probably at least as high, especially if the "protection money" paid to the police is counted. This includes free food and drink that is given to them because they are "friends" rather than because it is directly solicited. Despite these costs and the risks involved, however, beer trade prospers

2. This is probably a conservative estimate.

because it is the only way that many people can earn money to live.

Strength of symbols of community

Highly affective condensation symbols particularly identified with a community can help increase the sense of identity participants feel. The symbols per se are not important; their effectiveness lies in the ways in which people respond to them (Edelman 1964:chap. 1). For example, in Kenya at the time of independence the symbols of *uhuru* and Kenyatta were particularly effective in producing high levels of positive affect among the mass of the population and in increasing identification with the nation. The power of any symbol can vary quite rapidly, and, as many African political leaders have learned in the post-independence period, at times there may be no symbols which are particularly effective in evoking positive response from the public. The power of a symbol lies in its ability to prompt the quick and simple definition of a community as distinct, usually more in the affective than in the instrumental sense (Cobb and Elder 1972). Such symbols as "African socialism," for example, have consistently had relatively little specific meaning aside from the emotional responses they evoke.

In Mathare 2 there are two types of affective symbols which contribute to the development of a sense of community. There are local symbols such as the social hall and the village leaders, which set the population of the community apart from the wider society. Other symbols are not uniquely associated with the community, but are nonetheless used by the leaders to stress the common bonds between the area residents. These are the symbols of Kikuyu politics and the independence struggle, which are still particularly meaningful to these people, in contrast to most other Nairobi residents.

The most important symbols which stress the uniqueness or distinctiveness of Mathare 2 are related to concrete achievements and successes, such as the nursery school, the social hall, the savings and credit cooperative, and the water project. Thus the existence and successful operation of community institutions generates symbols of identification which increase the sense of community. Another group of symbols is associated with the conditions of squatter life in the area; these identify the community in terms of *pombe*, poor housing, poverty, and social ostracism.

The affective symbols not uniquely associated with the community stress the independence struggle and the Emergency experience, which is so important in the lives of most older and middle-aged Kikuyus. Most of the older residents and village leaders in Mathare spent from two to seven years in British detention camps because of alleged involvement with Mau Mau. Many younger residents lost one or both of their parents, and almost everyone felt the effects of the regulation of movement and of British colonial control. Following this experience came their participation in the political independence movement in the early 1960s. While many of the specific promises directed toward people like themselves, such as free land and free education, have not been met, in general Mathare residents see conditions as far better than before and are among the strongest supporters of President Jomo Kenyatta. In early 1969, when groups of Kikuyu came to Kenyatta's farm at Gatundu to pledge their loyalty to the president and to contribute money to the KANU campaign chest in an oathing ceremony which some said reminded them of the Mau Mau rites, residents from Mathare were among the first to arrive.

Thus in Mathare 2 there is a wide range of affective symbols which contribute to the sense of community in the area. The exact strength of their contribution to the development of a sense of community is difficult to assess. They do not seem to be nearly as crucial as either of the first two variables considered—the perceived importance of the community in people's lives and the level of outside threat.

Participation in community activities and rituals

Individual participation in specific social and political activities and rituals increases individual identification with a group or community (Verba 1961). *Rites de passage,* voting, and participation in decision-making at community meetings all enhance common identification, providing a common bond between the individual and other members in a community and separating them from outsiders. Through their participation they not only reaffirm their commitment to the community, but also strengthen the community's institutions and customs.

Participation does not necessarily have to be orderly or harmonious for feelings of community to be strengthened. In fact, as Gluckman (1966) and Coser (1956) have pointed out, the playing out of conflicts through established norms and institutions gives individuals an opportunity to reaffirm their acceptance of these norms and, in turn, the legitimacy of the community itself. Thus the presence of participation opportunities and the level of involvement is likely to be somewhat more important than the specific forms which participation takes.

TABLE 7.5 PARTICIPATION IN VILLAGE POLITICAL INSTITUTIONS IN MATHARE 2*

Activity	Yes	No
Have you ever:		
attended a village meeting?	89%	11%
voted in a village election?	88	12
paid the youth wing monthly dues?	90	10
taken a problem to a member of the village committee?	92	8
taken a problem to the village elders?	77	23
helped in a community building project?	93	7
Are you:		
a member of the social hall?	49	51
a member of the cooperative society?	30	70

*Sample size varies between 231 and 233.

In many urban neighborhoods there is low participation in local community activities, and typically many people are even unaware of most participation opportunities when they do exist.[3] In contrast, in Mathare 2 local participation levels are quite high, as is shown in Table 7.5. Although only a small group actually participates in decision-making, many more attend village meetings, vote in village elections, pay village assessments, take problems to village leaders or elders, work in a village project, or join a community organization. Thus residents of Mathare 2 have high rates of community participation both in formal political institutions and through more informal channels.

Conclusions

The sense of community in Mathare 2 is a function of the perceived importance of the community in participants' lives, the level of threats to participation and membership in the community, the existence of highly affective symbols of community, and the level of participation in local activities and rituals, as is summarized in Table 7.6. The relative importance of each of these independent variables is a question to be considered in the final chapter, after all the variables explaining political integration have been presented. The four variables considered in this chapter are also related to the growth of community institutions, and their inclusion in the discussion of sense of community does not deny this relationship. Along with the indicators for each variable, Table 7.6 also presents a score for each. This score represents an implicit comparison of Mathare 2 with other Nairobi neighborhoods, and considers as well the estimated potential range of variation possible on a given indicator. The perceived importance of the community and level of participation are both scored high, while threats to participation and the existence of affective symbols are scored medium/high,

3. A number of hypotheses relating the type of neighborhood to forms and levels of participation in the city are found in Greer (1962:chaps. 3 and 4).

TABLE 7.6 SUMMARY OF VARIABLES EXPLAINING SENSE OF COMMUNITY IN MATHARE 2

Variable	Indicators	Score
Perceived importance of the community in people's lives	Level of alternatives as measured by lack of land in rural areas, absence of skills for urban jobs, and dependence on Mathare location for economic subsistence, particularly in beer brewing	High
Threats to participation and membership in the community	Ostracism and stigmatization of wider society	Medium
	Police raids and threats of intervention due to illegal beer-brewing activities and illegal status of community	Medium/ High
Existence of affective symbols of community	Symbols associated particularly with the local community, such as social hall or squatting	Medium
	Symbols not exclusively associated with local community but important in uniting people, such as Kikuyu Emergency experience	High
Participation in community activities and rituals	Level of participation in village meetings and elections, payment of assessments, taking a problem to leaders or elders, working on a village project, and joining a village organization	High

as it is clear that threat could be greatly increased (even to the point where community organization and identity would be destroyed), and while affective symbols of the community are present, the residents do not feel as strongly about them as they might.

154

8

Strength of community institutions in Mathare 2

When do people living in an area build community institutions to manage and regulate interaction within their community and to confront jointly problems which community participants have in common? In most communities in the world this question is not relevant, as people find themselves born into a community which already has a set of functioning institutions. In a few cases, however, the growth and development of community institutions take place in a relatively short period of time. In Mathare 2, in a few years in the mid-1960s, the range of community institutions described in chapter 6 was created. To explain this process we consider, in addition to the sense of community, the following variables proposed in an earlier chapter: (1) the degree of social and cultural homogeneity; (2) the proportion of interaction within the community; (3) the level of mutual interdependence between community participants; (4) the level of institutional generalizability, or spillover potential; and (5) the level of social-emotional and task skills of community leaders.

Social and cultural homogeneity

Social and cultural homogeneity is the extent to which community participants have common backgrounds and perceive themselves as distinct from people in other communities in terms of their social and cultural experiences. Jacob and Teune hypothesize that

> social homogeneity will contribute strongly to the feasibility of political integration and, conversely, that communities whose members are very different from one another will have a hard time achieving or maintaining political integration. (1964:18)

They point out, however, that social homogeneity can be measured in a variety of ways. They identify ten factors:

> wealth or income, education, status or class, religion, race, language, ethnic identification, attitudes (a catch-all of different types of dispositional factors such as perceptions, fears, aspirations, loyalties), values, and "character" (which in the sense of social or communal character is taken to be a composite of traits held to distinguish a particular group). (1964:18–19)

Homogeneity means that the members of the community not only share some characteristic, but also that the characteristic is defined in each specific social context rather than in abstract terms. In western Kenya, for example, there is a sharp distinction made between the Luo and Baluhya, the two major tribal groups in the area. In Kampala, the capital of Uganda, several hundred miles away, the social distance between them is often much less, because of their common "outsider" status (Parkin 1969). Members of a community perceive ways in which they are more similar to one another than they are to nonmembers. In western Kenya, the Luo and Baluhya tend to acknowledge similarity only to their own tribal communities. In the urban context of Kampala, a different situation is created by their common status as Kenyans, who are rejected for jobs if there are Ugandans available, and who find that they have more in common with one another than they do with members of some of the Uganda tribes.

Perhaps the most useful way to consider homogeneity is to

talk about what Deutsch et al. (1957) call "a distinctive way of life" that is shared by community members. This is particularly relevant in small communities, where the everyday routines and face-to-face contacts of members are likely to emphasize the characteristics they share and the ways in which they are different from outsiders. In urban neighborhoods, or rural communities in which members have a high level of contact with outsiders, these feelings are often likely to be reinforced, and the distinctive way of life refers to a number of shared characteristics not held by outsiders.

In Mathare 2 a number of different factors contribute to the development of a distinctive way of life. The most visible and obvious difference from outsiders is Mathare's reliance on the *pombe* economy. Table 7.2 dramatically illustrates the great differences between Mathare's population and that of Shauri Moyo and Kariokor. In addition, the homogeneity of Mathare's population can be considered in terms of their migration and urban experience, ethnicity, and household and family structure.

Migration and urban experience

The residents of Mathare Village 2, for the most part, are not newcomers to the urban area, although almost all of them are migrants to the city. The most common pattern, as Table 8.1 shows, is for a person to have been born in a rural community, to have lived several years in another neighborhood in Nairobi, and then to have moved into Mathare. Only 2 per cent of the adult population of the village were born in Nairobi, although they have spent an average of eleven years living in the city. (The average age of the sample is thirty-two.) About one-quarter of the population report that they moved to Mathare directly from a rural community, and that their average length of residence in the village was between three and four years.

In terms of migration experience and length of residence in the city, the people living in Mathare are not very different

TABLE 8.1 Comparison of Migration and Urban Experience of Mathare Residents and Other Nairobi Africans

| | BIRTHPLACE | |
	Mathare Residents	Nairobi Sample
Nairobi	2%	4%
Outside Nairobi	98	96
	100%	100%
Sample size	233	498
	RESIDENCE PRIOR TO PRESENT NEIGHBORHOOD	
	Mathare Residents	Nairobi Sample
Other neighborhood in Nairobi	75%	53%
Outside Nairobi	25	47
	100%	100%
Sample size	197	86
	LENGTH OF RESIDENCE IN NAIROBI	
	Mathare Residents	Nairobi Sample
0–2 years	8%	21%
3–5 years	19	28
6–10 years	42	17
11 years or more	31	34
	100%	100%
Mean number of years in city	10.7	9.5
Mean percentage of life in city	33.2%	28.9%
Sample size	233	496
	NUMBER OF YEARS IN PRESENT NEIGHBORHOOD	
	Mathare Residents	Nairobi Sample
1 year or less	7%	28%
2 years	22	18

TABLE 8.1 CONTINUED

| | BIRTHPLACE | |
	Mathare Residents	Nairobi Sample
3 years	17	19
4 years	25	14
5 years	28	20
	99%	99%
Sample size	234	495

from other Africans living in Nairobi. If anything, they appear to have spent a greater portion of their lives in the city, although the differences are very small. What is clear, however, is that Mathare is not simply a "first stop" in the migration process or a "waiting room" where the latest wave of immigrants are located until they begin to improve their positions in the city. On the contrary, they have lived in the city and neighborhood longer than people in other neighborhoods; their status as squatters, therefore, can hardly be seen as a temporary aspect of the urban socialization process. Similar findings were reported in studies conducted in squatter communities in other areas of the world (Mangin 1967:68).

Mathare residents, then, are generally migrants to the city who have lived elsewhere in Nairobi before moving to the community. Despite their urban experience, the residents of Mathare still maintain strong ties with relatives living in the rural areas, although not as strong as those maintained by other Africans in the city. About two-thirds of the Mathare residents report that they have visited relatives in the rural areas at least once during the past year, that they received relatives from home in the city during the past year, and that they sent money home to rural relatives. About 80 per cent of the other Nairobi Africans engaged in each of these types of rural contact.

159

Ethnicity

Four tribal groups—the Kikuyu, Kamba, Luo, and Baluhya—make up 90 per cent of the African population of Nairobi. In Village 2, 87 per cent of the population are Kikuyu, and, among the other three groups, only the Kamba are found in any proportion comparable to their representation in the entire city, as is shown in Table 8.2. Mathare's tribal homogeneity is striking, but not unique, as there are other neighborhoods in Nairobi where the concentration of residents from one tribe

TABLE 8.2 COMPARISON OF TRIBE AND PLACE OF BIRTH OF MATHARE
RESIDENTS AND OTHER NAIROBI AFRICANS

	TRIBE	
	Mathare Residents	Nairobi (1969 census)
Kikuyu	86%	47%
Kamba	11	14
Baluhya	1	16
Luo	1	15
Other	2	7
	101%	99%
Sample size	233	—

	PLACE OF BIRTH	
	Mathare Residents	Nairobi* (1962 census)
Kiambu District	38%	10%
Fort Hall	28	18
Nyeri	13	8
Nyanza Province	1	14
Western Province	1	14
Machakos	9	13
Kitui	2	4
Other	8	19
	100%	100%
Sample size	233	16,909

*The 1969 census is more recent but the published figures do not distinguish between the birthplace of adults and children, which is crucial in the comparison here. The figures in the table come from a 10 per cent sample of the 1962 census kindly provided to the author by the Statistics Division of the Ministry of Economic Development and Planning.

(often the Kikuyu, who are the largest single group in the city) or the absence of one or two groups is as marked as it is in Mathare.

The Kikuyu domination of the community is noticeable, although at times the leaders go to great lengths in saying the village is "tribally mixed," meaning that there are a few non-Kikuyus living there. Kikuyu is the major language spoken in the village, and there are many people whose knowledge of any other language is rudimentary, although they are usually able to conduct very simple conversations and marketing in Swahili, and virtually all of the records are kept in Swahili. This, of course, poses a problem to any non-Kikuyu in the community. For the Kamba, however, the difficulties are not as severe as for other groups. Kamba is very similar to Kikuyu in grammatical structure, pronunciation, and vocabulary, so that there are many people in Nairobi for whom the two languages are mutually intelligible after a relatively short time. That is, when a Kikuyu and a Kamba meet, each may speak his own language and be understood by the other. In addition, many Kamba in Nairobi learn to speak Kikuyu fairly well, although few Kikuyu bother to learn to speak Kamba.[1] It is not clear whether this is related to the relative dominance of the Kikuyu in Nairobi, or to more fundamental attitudes on the part of each tribe about its own language.[2]

Kikuyu circumcision ceremonies are regularly held in the village in December, and other institutions associated with Kikuyu tradition are found there. People are very conscious of the "traditional way of doing things" and are generally respectful of tradition. The community is not, however, simply a rural village re-created in the center of a modern city. Not only are individuals far less isolated from outsiders than they would be

1. Note that language attitudes in this case, as in many others, are not reciprocal (see Wolff 1964).
2. A common attitude in Nairobi is the resistance of the Kikuyu to speaking Swahili, and their lukewarm attitude toward making it the Kenya national language.

in a rural setting, but the links between individuals and families are of an entirely different order. In a traditional rural community, individuals are in face-to-face contact from birth, and are able to find a wide system of personal and social ties that bind them together. No comparable ties exist in a new community such as Mathare, where most of the residents did not know each other before moving to the village.[3]

Household and family structure

In contrast to other neighborhoods in Nairobi, women constitute an overwhelming majority of the adult population in Mathare. In 1962 there were about two adult men for every woman in the African population of the city as a whole, while in Mathare at the time of the study the figures were reversed. As is shown in Table 8.3, these differences are most striking among the

TABLE 8.3 COMPARISON OF HOUSEHOLD AND FAMILY STRUCTURE OF MATHARE RESIDENTS AND OTHER NAIROBI AFRICANS

| | SEX | |
	Mathare Residents	Nairobi Sample
Male	34%	66%
Female	66	34
	100%	100%
Sample size	234	498

| | AGE GROUP BY SEX | | | |
| | Mathare residents | | Nairobi Sample | |
	Male	Female	Male	Female
20–30 years	39%	60%	34%	56%
31–40	43	33	40	26
41 and older	18	7	27	18
	100%	100%	101%	100%
Sample size	79	153	330	168

3. For a discussion of this same point regarding Latin American communities, see Mangin (1967:80–82).

TABLE 8.3 CONTINUED

| | MARITAL STATUS | |
	Mathare Residents	Nairobi Sample
Single	33%	26%
Married and living with spouse	25	45
Married and spouse living outside Nairobi	9	25
Separated or divorced	17	1
Widowed	16	3
	100%	100%
Sample size	234	497
	NUMBER OF CHILDREN	
	Mathare Residents	Nairobi Sample
0	37%	31%
1	11	10
2	17	13
3	13	12
4 or more	22	34
	100%	100%
Sample size	229	498
	RESIDENCE OF CHILDREN	
	Mathare Residents	Nairobi Sample
Residing in Nairobi with parent	82%	56%
Residing outside Nairobi	18	44
	100%	100%
Sample size	427	1,280

twenty- to thirty-year-olds in Mathare, although the ratios of men to women *within* each age group are roughly similar in both samples.

The residents of Mathare are generally young, and living without a mate. Only a quarter of the sample reports being married and living with a spouse in the city, although the majority have one or two small children who must be supported. This becomes extremely difficult, as so few people in the community have the skills to earn a living in the city. Mathare residents are far less educated, less skilled, and consequently less able to find permanent employment than people in other parts of the city. This is particularly true for women, as data show that less than 10 per cent in Mathare have completed primary school. Thus, even in situations where a person from Mathare can find work, it is almost invariably the most menial and the lowest paying sort of job.

Within the context of Nairobi, Mathare is characterized by a distinctive life-style. Its most visible distinction lies in its extreme marginality and dependence on beer brewing and other subsistence activities. Other data reveal the community's distinctiveness in ethnicity and in household and family structure. In terms of migration and urban experience, however, Mathare 2 is not particularly distinguishable from other areas of the city. Social and cultural homogeneity in the community contributes to the development of community-wide institutions for two reasons: (1) it increases the social trust among residents who see themselves as distinctive, thus enhancing the possibilities for cooperative action, and (2) because individuals see themselves as having the same social characteristics as their neighbors, they are more likely to feel that they share common problems, and that these problems are subject to common solutions.

Interaction patterns

High levels of interaction within a community are likely to be accompanied by demands on community institutions which regulate and order the interactions. Increasing interaction and communication within a community are indications of what Deutsch et al. (1957) call increasing salience or mutual awareness; this may entail the development of specific institutions which regularize and manage interaction, such as a post office or village council meetings. Conversely, the level of interaction within a community can diminish over time, as people develop new ways of doing things. The loss of autonomy and control in local rural communities throughout the world is related to a weakening of local political institutions and to a decrease in local interactions, in proportion to all interactions (Vidich and Bensman 1960). Local institutions lose importance as people are increasingly tied into a wide set of relationships and as communities become less isolated and self-sufficient (Wilson and Wilson 1965; van Hoey 1968).

Social and economic conditions create a higher level of interdependence within Mathare Village 2 than is found in most other neighborhoods in Nairobi. Individuals living in the community spend a greater proportion of their time in the village than do people in other areas. Few people hold jobs that take them out of the Mathare area daily. In addition, the pattern of economic subsistence leads to close cooperation between neighbors and to frequent pooling of meager resources. Finally, the tribal homogeneity of the community and the common past political experiences create an atmosphere in which most of the residents feel comfortable.

One consequence is that a majority of the people in Village 2 say that their closest friend in Nairobi is living in their neighborhood, in contrast to other areas in the city where barely a quarter made the same statement, as shown in Table 8.4. Furthermore, although more men than women in both samples said their best friend lived in a different neighborhood, the differences between men and women were more pronounced in other parts of the city than in Mathare. In the other neighborhoods, men are much more likely to work outside the neighborhood than are women, who are more prone to stay home with their children; in Mathare, both men and women are likely to spend most of their day in the community, although the majority leave the community daily for brief periods of time.

TABLE 8.4 COMPARISON OF LOCATION OF CLOSEST FRIENDS AMONG MATHARE
RESIDENTS AND OTHER NAIROBI AFRICANS

| | Mathare | | | Nairobi | | |
	Men	Women	Total	Men	Women	Total
Closest friend in:						
Same neighborhood	47%	54%	52%	21%	30%	24%
Different neighborhood	53	46	48	79	70	76
	100%	100%	100%	100%	100%	100%
Sample size	76	147	223	316	158	474

Mutual interdependence

Mutual interdependence refers to the degree to which one portion of a community relies upon the goods and services of another portion. Increases in mutual interdependence mean a lowering of autonomy within the community and are often accompanied by the development of additional institutions, or the expansion of existing ones. High levels of mutual interdependence can be seen in the operation of any modern economic system, or in the operation of the role system in any traditional village. In both cases, one part of the community finds itself dependent on the activities and interests of another part. Mutual interdependence increases people's opportunities for achievement of goals which require the contributions of individuals or groups with different skills, and, at the same time, increases their dependence on other people in their day-to-day existence. In urban communities this mutual dependence is often not seen on a face-to-face level. Rather, urbanites depend on the "invisible hand" of the market, of government agencies such as the schools, health agencies, and the police, and of private agencies such as light and power companies. All these have great importance to an individual city dweller, as the stoppage of any one quickly reveals.

In Mathare 2, mutual interdependence is seen in the cooperation between village residents involved in beer brewing and other subsistence economic activities. A relatively common arrangement is for several women to go into business together. They share the costs of the raw materials, divide the brewing tasks, and split the final profits. In addition to sharing the work involved in the beer brewing and selling, they also assist each other in the care and feeding of their children. Thus in a "business" involving three women, two may be working on the brewing while the third takes care of all the children. Similarly, there are several possible arrangements regarding the selling. They may divide the beer between them in order to try to sell it as quickly as possible, or one or two of the women may be in charge of selling at any one time while the other is stationed near the road to alert the sellers in case the police come. The result is very close cooperation between several women, who act as one "household" in terms of economic activities, preparation of food, and child-rearing. Such cooperation is clearly important to women who risk arrest, as they know that there will be someone to take care of their children until they can return.

Another form of mutual interdependence is that which exists between Mathare and the larger urban setting of Nairobi. The location of the community, as previously discussed, is vital, since the *pombe* economy would lack a market if it were not for customers from neighboring communities. Thus interdependence exists within the community, but also between Mathare and other parts of the city.

Institutional generalizability (spillover potential)

Institutional generalizability is the extent to which institutions operating in one sphere are capable of undertaking tasks in another. For example, in some cultural settings it is relatively easy for a religious organization to assume political or military functions, while in others this task expansion or spillover into other sectors is difficult if not impossible (Nye 1970). On both the national and international levels it has been far easier to organize the fast and efficient distribution of mail than to redistribute wealth. Many effective community-wide institutions are well suited for taking on additional tasks and handling them successfully. However, Haas suggests that there are situations where leaders are interested in institutional expansion, and where the organizations are capable of such a change, but where it does not come about. In studying the International Labor Organization (ILO), he found that the diffuseness and heterogeneity of the international system and the low level of feedback between the international and national levels led to less task expansion and growth than he had initially hypothesized (Haas 1964:459).

One of the crucial aspects of institutional growth is that institutions must be relatively strong at the outset and must grow at a faster pace than the demands made on them during the early stages. Deutsch says, "Rewards must come before the penalties, and rewards must be strong and frequent enough to initiate the habit" (1964:55)—the "habit" being the shifting of allegiance to the new community. In short, institutions must show what Deutsch calls a high level of "political responsiveness."

Spillover potential can be considered an attitudinal predisposition within a community, a rejection of the idea that the tasks which community institutions perform must be carefully spelled out and are relatively difficult to expand. In Mathare 2, the apparent attitude of residents is that the community leaders and institutions ought to involve themselves in questions of the welfare of people living in the community. Exactly what specific problems are considered and the manner in which community action is taken are relatively open-ended. The expansion of village organizations—from the KANU branch, working for the election of specific candidates in the independence period, to the present range of institutions—in a few years is a result of this attitude. A desk drawer in the village office in Mathare

2 contains three rubber stamps—one for the KANU branch, one for the social hall, and one for the savings and credit cooperative. The officers of each of these organizations and, in fact, of other community organizations as well, are virtually identical. They are not particularly concerned with functional differentiation between the tasks of the different organizations, and generally they make little effort to specify whether their actions are taking place under the rubric of one or the other.

One aspect of spillover which should be noted is the implicit legitimation of the Mathare institutions and leaders by Kenya government officials, ranging from the district officers to police officials to bureaucrats in specific central government and city agencies. Whenever they arrive in the community, government officials generally look for the village leaders, and Kiboro in particular, to help them in handling whatever problem brought them to Mathare. They also sanction specific projects such as the construction of the nursery school or the collection of funds for the water project, thus giving explicit recognition to the legitimacy of community activities, if not of the community itself. Government officials recognize the importance of having clearly defined leaders and effective institutions in the community; they understand that the absence of leaders and the destruction of community institutions would make the performance of their own jobs more difficult. Thus they come to be partially responsible for the generation of an attitude favorable to institutional generalization, since they sanction existing activities and rarely oppose task expansion.

Leadership skills

Leadership skills refer to the ability of community leaders to perform well in office, as judged by the people in the community. The skills associated with successful leadership can be either technical or social-emotional in nature, and their specific content will vary across situations. In some contexts the good leader remains aloof from the community, while in other settings he participates in all community activities. Both technical and social-emotional skills are required in most communities; they may be found in a single leader or there may be several leaders in the community, each with complementary skills.

Poor leaders weaken the community institutions in a variety of ways. Leaders lacking technical skills weaken support for the institutions because they are unable to render the services expected of them. Corrupt leaders weaken support for institutions because people come to associate the corruption with both the leaders and the institutions. Colorless leaders, who are unable to provide emotional leadership, weaken the institutions by failing to strengthen people's affective attachments to the community.

Mathare Valley Village 2 is extremely well organized, not only for a squatter area, but in comparison with other local neighborhoods in Nairobi or in other large cities in the world. There are well-defined leadership positions in the community and in the village-wide political institutions, and these are operating on a more or less regular basis. The leaders' authority is defined through their own interaction with the villagers, since only one of the institutions, the cooperative society, has any clearly recognized legal standing as far as the governments of Kenya or Nairobi are concerned. On the other hand, while the government officially recognizes niether the right of the villagers to live in Mathare nor the decisions of the village committee, it does unofficially recognize and support the village leaders. It has found that the presence of clearly defined village authorities who cooperate with government officials from time to time is preferable to a situation of anarchy.

In the village there are six community-wide political institutions: the village committee, the social hall committee, the committee of elders, the savings and credit cooperative, the local KANU branch, and the youth wing. In practice, the leaders of all except the youth wing are the same people, and the functions of each of the institutions are not always clearly defined and separated. At times it is possible to tell which group is meeting only by the rubber stamp that is placed on the minutes of the meeting. For example, the village committee is theoretically chosen by all the people living in the village, while the social hall committee is selected only by those people who have joined the social hall. However, almost all of the members of the village committee have been elected to the social hall committee, and in their village meetings problems dealing with the social hall are not usually separated from general village problems.

The oldest residents of the community report that a village committee was first formed in the early 1960s to try to prevent the government from bulldozing the community and to support certain KANU candidates in the pre-independence political struggles. The first village leaders, called Wango and Kihigi Gichoi, have since bought land in the rural areas and are no longer living in Nairobi. Zipporah Wainina, the first head of the women, still lives in the community and serves on the village committee. At about the time of independence, in 1963, E. W. Kiboro, the present leader, became chairman of the village. The other leaders at the time of this study were: Gathoni Mbuthia, head of the women; Kariuki Gichohi, vice-chairman; and W. Gitau Gachukia, secretary. Their participation in leadership positions in each of the institutions is determined by their availability, interest, and skills. For example, the vice-chairman is in charge of the committee of elders and chairs most of the meetings when cases are heard, while the secretary does most of the work for the cooperative society.

Without a doubt, the single most important person in the village is the chairman, "Ndururu" Kiboro. His abilities as a leader and organizer are extraordinary, and he is responsible for almost all of the important decisions the village committees make. He chairs all meetings whenever he is present, talks more than anyone else, and continually oversees the work of others in the village. Of tremendous importance to his success as leader is the wide range of contacts he has with politicians, administrators, and businessmen in Nairobi and Kiambu. When problems arise that he is not able to solve, he knows whom to go to for assistance, and how to approach him. His contacts have been tremendously important in gaining informal promises from the government that the community will not be bulldozed, in getting school fees remitted for many villagers, and in obtaining government encouragement for many village development projects.

Informants reported that the village leaders are selected every four years through a complicated electoral procedure which involves the direct selection of a leader for the men and one for the women, the nomination by the designated leaders of an equal number of men and women to serve on the village committee, and their selection in a general election presided over by the Member of Parliament for the area. I did not observe such an election, and I suspect that this description probably represents an idealization of a simpler process.

The leaders' authority within the community rests on their ability to induce compliance with their decisions, as they have no formal powers to insure enforcement, and their informal powers of persuasion are often limited. For example, it was reported to me that the village chairman would not pay the fines for anyone arrested for beer brewing or selling unless they were members of the social hall. This was probably important in inducing some women to join the social hall, but might make relatively little difference to those not involved in the beer business.

The village leaders are different from most other people in Mathare in several important respects, as shown in Table 8.5. They are older, more likely to have lived in Nairobi for a long period of time, more likely to have lived in Mathare before the Emergency, and more likely to have spent some time in a detention camp during the Emergency. At the same time, they are less educated, less likely to be employed, and less likely to own land in the rural areas. They also have lower incomes than nonleaders in the community. Thus a leader in the village is likely to be a relatively long-term city resident, often with ties in Mathare going back as many as twenty years, who is unable to find urban employment, has an extremely low monthly income, and has no real rural alternative today.

TABLE 8.5 COMPARISON OF URBAN EXPERIENCE AND SOCIAL STATUS OF LEADERS AND NONLEADERS IN MATHARE*

	Leaders		Nonleaders	
More than 30 years old	100%	(15)	44%	(219)
Lived in Nairobi more than ten years	73	(15)	28	(219)
Mathare resident before Emergency	33	(15)	10	(219)
Detained during Emergency	73	(15)	27	(219)
Unemployed	87	(15)	53	(217)
No formal education	80	(15)	54	(215)
Landless	93	(15)	72	(219)
Income below Shs. 200/ - monthly	87	(15)	67	(212)

*Sample sizes are given in parentheses.

The village leaders are highly visible in the community. The social hall and village offices are located in the center of the area and are a focus of movement and activity throughout the day and night. Furthermore, the fact that so few of the village leaders have any regular activities outside of the valley means that they are continually seen. The village offices are almost always open and people frequently come to seek information or assistance. Thus, in addition to the tangible services which the village leaders have provided, such as the water supply, the nursery school, and the social hall, they also provide informal services to many members of the community.

One of the most important services that the village leaders render is mediation between people in the community and the bureaucratic structures in the wider society. As was pointed out earlier, most of the people in Mathare are particularly ill-prepared for life in a modern city. When problems come up, they often have no idea what to do, other than to ask a village leader for advice or assistance. Several cases described below give some idea of the kinds of problems for which people seek help.

> Three women came to the office one day and told the village secretary that they heard that other women in the village were getting free milk for their children and they wondered if they could get some also. He explained that the Eastleigh Community Centre, located nearby, was supplying free milk daily and told them how they could send their children every day to get milk too.

> A young man came into the office and asked the village secretary to help him fill out a job application in English because he felt that if it was in English he would have a better chance of being employed by the company. The village secretary helped him and then typed the letter using the village typewriter.

> A woman came to the office and explained that she had a court case coming up charging a young man in the village with getting her daughter pregnant. She explained to the village leaders the damages that she was seeking in the suit and asked them to help her. The secretary said that he thought that she would not get all that she was seeking, but she was adamant about not lowering her demands. He wrote them all down and typed them on a form which was then submitted to the court.

In each of these cases people in the community came to the village office to seek help in coping with the wider society, which they do not understand especially well. In some cases, of course, the village leaders can provide only a small amount of assistance; for example, the young man in the second case did not get the job he wanted. In most situations their efforts to help others serve to strengthen their visibility.

The mediating role of the village leaders is particularly important in dealing with specific government agencies or authorities. The village chairman is especially fit for this role because of his wide range of political contacts throughout Nairobi and his knowledge of whom to approach with what problem. The following case illustrates this very clearly.

There was a fire in the village one night which started when a man got drunk and had a fight with the woman he was living with; in the process, he knocked over a kerosene lantern in the room, setting it and neighboring rooms afire. Before the blaze could be put out, eight rooms were completely destroyed and thirteen others were damaged. That night the homeless stayed either with friends or in the social hall. In the morning, Kiboro called the district officer for permission to rebuild the rooms that were destroyed in the fire. In the afternoon the district officer inspected the area, but he wanted to wait for a few days before deciding how many houses could be rebuilt. However, Kiboro kept pressing him, in front of a crowd of villagers who had gathered to watch. He argued that the people would have no place to go, that the government had a responsibility to allow them to rebuild their rooms, and that they were all loyal KANU followers. The district officer accepted this, but he and Kiboro had difficulty agreeing on how many rooms could be rebuilt. Again, after extensive prodding, he acceded to Kiboro's request, giving permission for twelve new rooms to be built in the village. The onlooking villagers smiled at one another throughout the discussion between Kiboro and the government official.

Government officials, such as the district officer, admit that Kiboro's presence in the village makes their jobs easier. He helps keep order in the community and enforces government regulations. Furthermore, when an official has something to communicate to the village, he finds that he can speak to Kiboro and have the information transmitted to the people. In addition, governmental orders, such as those against building additional houses in the village, are generally enforced by Kiboro and the village committee, but more in terms of the spirit than the letter of the law. Once the district officer visited the village and ordered several rooms destroyed, charging that they had been built without authorization. An old lady, unable to work and without money, lived in one of them. As soon as the officer left the village, Kiboro ordered several people to help build another room for her, saying that the community would pay the expenses. The leaders explained that the district officer would not make another inspection for five or six months and that it was worth the risk.

Kiboro is one of the few people in the village who can successfully intervene with government officials. He is extremely good at making his arguments specific, clear, and strong. Virtually no one else in the village could have obtained permission, for example, to build new rooms in the community after the fire. The public aspect of this particular type of confrontation is especially important in enhancing the prestige of the village leaders, and in reinforcing the belief that they are capable of getting things done for the community. Interestingly, despite the fact that Kiboro secured permission to rebuild the rooms within twenty-four hours after the fire, no work was undertaken at all for several weeks. In some cases, this was because the victims decided to live elsewhere; in others, the owners of the rooms were not around at the time; and for everyone there was the problem of getting the money to buy the materials needed for rebuilding.

The village chairman, through his knowledge of government officials and the political structure of the capital, provides services for people that they are unable to provide for themselves. Before the opening of the school term in Nairobi, he visits with schoolmasters on behalf of the village and parents, trying to get children from the village accepted into government schools and seeking tuition remissions so that the parents can afford to send them. This means that he must attend the meetings of a large number of school committees and try to convince each one of them of the worthiness of every case he brings before them. The alternative for a parent is either paying the school fees or trying to present the case himself in a situation with which he is likely to be totally unfamiliar.

The role of the leaders in the village is most important in serving as intermediaries in cases arising from beer brewing and selling. When police conduct a raid in the village, they generally inform the village leader and allow him to visit those who have been arrested. In addition, he is often able to speak to the officers in charge of the raid and to limit the number of people they arrest by convincing them to release certain people whom he says he knows well. Finally, Kiboro generally goes to the court for the trial and sentencing, and pays the fines if the convicted villagers have no money with them.

Another type of intervention with the police serves to help limit the seeking of bribes and other abuses on the part of constables. Because the leaders know the police officers well, they can speak to them about abuses. If this produces no change in the behavior of a particular constable or group of constables, they may then make a formal appeal to government officials, such as the letter to a local Member of Parliament shown in Figure 8.1.

FIGURE 8.1 LETTER TO THE HONORABLE DR. F. M. WAIYAKI

KANU Mathare Valley
Nairobi
26 February 1968

The Hon. Dr. F. M. Waiyaki
North East Division,
Nairobi

Dear Sir:

Re: *Grievances of Mathare Valley*

I have the honour to bring the following complaints to our government for help:

The people living in Mathare are greatly disturbed by the police when they come to arrest people in each village. We are not complaining about those police constables doing their duty. We are talking about certain abuses.

(a) They often break into houses of the residents when they have gone to their jobs in Nairobi. After breaking in they leave the door unlocked, so that thieves can come and take the people's possessions.

(b) When they are arresting people, they don't always follow regulations. Sometimes when they find one tin (one pint) of *pombe*, they arrest between twenty and thirty people in the area. Other times they take people who are just walking along the street and charge them with being in possession of A.I.L. (African Intoxicating Liquor). Such people are never in a position to defend themselves.

(c) They are making a large amount of money from the Public by soliciting bribes of Shs. 20/- or more. This is done by only a few of the police constables when they are on duty and also when they are not on duty. They start arresting people but then they tell the people to buy them beer and/or pay them money.

(d) I therefore bring to our Government's attention these grievances. The present time is worse than the Emergency to the *wananchi* of Mathare Valley.

In the above circumstances I request the Government on behalf of the community to please look into the above matter and see if something can be done to avoid these illegal police actions which are now being carried out.

E. W. Ndururu Kiboro

The leadership's abilities to handle a wide range of problems and to retain the support of the people in the community are tremendously important in explaining the strength of institutions in Mathare 2. The leaders clearly have specific skills and political contacts allowing them to handle substantive problems quite effectively, particularly in comparison with the way in which individual residents would act if forced to rely on their own devices. Kiboro, in particular, has social-emotional skills as well, which allow him to cajole, convince, and, in the end, mobilize villagers to action.

It is tempting, in fact, to single out leadership skills as a single variable which might account for the high level of integration in Mathare 2, in comparison with other areas of Nairobi and with other villages in the Mathare area. Mathare 2 appeared to be the most integrated of the four villages in the area at the time of the study, and Kiboro and the other leaders seemed more forceful and capable than the heads of other villages. Yet on the basis of scattered observation in each of the other three communities, it appeared that additional factors were also responsible for the differences between them.

Leadership is indeed important, but even given the great variation in the four communities, all of them seemed more integrated than *any* other African neighborhoods I visited in Nairobi (with the exceptions of Kibera and Langata—squatter settlements in the western part of the city). Leadership seems to make some differences, but it can hardly by itself explain the presence or absence of organization. Another factor is the variation in social composition of the four communities. Village 3 was far more ethnically heterogeneous than Village 2; Village 4 was partially agricultural and dispersed; Village 1 seemed to be more faction-ridden. Systematic observation of all four communities, as well as other squatter settlements in the city, would be useful in attempting to better isolate those variables most crucial in the integration process. The likelihood of arriving at a single explanatory variable is small, however, given the complexity of social reality, and we shall turn in the final chapter to what we consider a more fruitful question: the interaction between the various independent variables.

Conclusions

The strength of community institutions in Mathare is a function of the social and cultural homogeneity of the community, the proportion of interactions within the community, the level of mutual interdependence between residents, the spillover

TABLE 8.6 SUMMARY OF VARIABLES EXPLAINING INSTITUTIONAL STRENGTH IN MATHARE 2

Variable	Indicator	Score
Social and cultural homogeneity (a distinctive way of life)	Distinctive life style associated with the *pombe* economy for squatters	High
	Economic marginality	High
	Migration and urban experience	Low
	Ethnicity	High
	Household and family structure	High
Level of interactions within the community (mutual relevance)	Friendship patterns	Medium
	Researcher's estimate of time spent within the community	Medium/high
Mutual interdependence between residents	Level of cooperation between residents in economic activity, child care	Medium/high
Institutional generalizability (spill-over potential)	Researcher's impression of the strength of attitudinal willingness to expand institutional tasks	High
	Governmental legitimation of community leaders and institutions, and encouragement of task expansion	Medium/high
Skills of leaders	Researcher's estimate of the social-emotional and task skills of community leaders	High

potential of community institutions, and the task and social-emotional skills of community leaders, as well as the sense of community in the area. Table 8.6 shows the specific indicators of each of these independent variables and the score, on a high-medium-low scale, for each. Before evaluating the contribution to integration of each of these variables and those considered in the previous chapter, we will briefly consider the ways in which political integration in a local community is distinctive.

9

Political integration
in local communities

In recent years political integration has been studied most extensively at the national and regional levels, while relatively few people have looked toward small communities for theoretical insights into the process. In Africa, small-community studies, mainly carried out by anthropologists in rural settings, have not been particularly concerned with the problems of community formation. Instead, they have tended to assume that such communities are and always have been highly integrated, that this integration rests upon traditional social and political organization, and that, therefore, questions concerning the creation of communities and the early stages of their integration are not particularly important. By combining the theoretical questions of political scientists interested in integration with those of anthropologists interested in local communities, we might begin to learn more about community integration, an aspect of politics in local units which is relatively unknown, and at the same time obtain a better understanding of the political integration process in general.[1]

There are local communities whose integration is independent

1. One important purpose in examining political integration at different levels is to get a more precise idea of which variables are important at all levels, and which seem to have particular importance at only one level. One empirical attempt in this direction is Cobb and Elder (1969), a comparison of international integration on the regional and global levels.

of traditional authority systems. The most obvious of these are the urban areas in Africa that are a relatively recent development in most parts of the continent (Gluckman 1960). The changing economies during the colonial period resulted in urban migrations, and while the colonial governments often made provision for administration of these areas, the African population was generally left on its own to determine in greater detail the specific nature of informal, and sometimes even formal, social control mechanisms within its communities. In some cases there was a borrowing of social institutions from the rural areas. Epstein (1958), for example, discusses the system of "tribal elders" that was used to represent workers on the Copperbelt. Such wholesale transplanting of social or political institutions from the rural to urban areas was, for the most part, unsuccessful.

The analysis of forces explaining political integration in Mathare 2 has not until now explicitly considered ways in which it might be different from integration at regional and national levels. When might integration be easier or more difficult to attain on one level than on another? What are the conditions which best account for these differences? In posing these questions with regard to Mathare 2, two variables in particular are considered: the effect of the small size of the community and the face-to-face character of interactions in the community, and the effect of the level of isolation or autonomy. How do they help explain the level of integration identified in Mathare 2?

Initial expectations

It is perfectly reasonable to expect Mathare 2, and similar urban areas, to be hardly integrated at all. It is not immediately obvious that a neighborhood in the larger urban community of Nairobi would have any community-wide political institutions. It is even less obvious that the structures would be relatively formalized and clearly defined, for it is not rare in Nairobi, or in most other cities in the world, to find neighborhoods where the sense of community is weak and community-wide political institutions virtually nonexistent.[2]

Small size, face-to-face interactions

In small communities characterized by face-to-face, rather than mediated, interactions, residents quickly develop relatively strong personal bonds (although not necessarily positive ones) to one another. Feedback is rapid and the mutual salience of actors is high. Probably the most striking aspect of life in such a community is the high visibility of people and events. Unlike situations at the international level, there is relatively little problem in attracting people's attention and in their seeing the relevance of a political institution to their own lives.

Mathare 2 is such a community. At the time of the study it had about 2,000 inhabitants, which makes it larger than many rural communities, but still not particularly large. Residents almost always deal with one another on a person-to-person, rather than on a mediated, basis. Much of their lives is not private. Houses are small and close together; cooperation becomes a necessity, and there are few well-kept secrets in the community. Almost everyone not only knows his neighbors, but also knows a great deal about them, although at the same time no one would claim to know everyone in the community. Economic life fosters further cooperation among women, and because of the continual threat of police raids, there is cooperation in selling, warning, and bribing. Isolated individuals—and they do exist—are at a

2. Greer (1962:98-99) discusses the relative independence of an individual from his local residential community in most urban settings: "The individual's investment is relatively small in the interactional network that constitutes the locality group, and if his losses are too great he can cut them by getting out—the community cannot hold him." At the same time, there is room for individual variation: "The local merchants have more of a stake than the home-owning residents with children, and these have more invested than the couple without children who rent an apartment. . . . However, even the most deeply involved can withdraw from the local community and satisfy all needs elsewhere—and the withdrawal need not be physical."

distinct disadvantage. One problem, of course, is to separate out the ways in which this cooperation is due to the face-to-face character of interactions as opposed to other variables, such as threat or social homogeneity.

One tentative conclusion might be that the political integration process, whether ultimately successful or unsuccessful, should be more rapid on the local level than on the national or international one, insofar as local conditions promote fast feedback and high visibility within the community. In Mathare 2, when the new nursery school was built in 1967, virtually everyone in the community either worked on it or knew about it before construction was finished. The same was true for the installation of the new water system. The high visibility of local leaders and institutions promotes rapid changes in sense of community and in the perceived effectiveness of local institutions. At the same time it should be pointed out that high visibility can also be disintegrative when it leads to demands which grow far more rapidly than capabilities. In Mathare 2 inhabitants have generally held such low expectations of the possibility of successful collective action that the successes have served to increase community integration.

A related hypothesis which suggests itself in evaluating the roots of political integration in Mathare 2 is that integration is mainly attributable to the ethnic homogeneity of the community—that it is primarily a result of the transplanting of rural and traditional Kikuyu institutions to an urban setting. Thus integration in Mathare may be susceptible of explanation in the same way as the integration of traditional Kikuyu communities. Although certainly intriguing, this hypothesis seems somewhat simplistic for several reasons. Most important is the fact that traditional rural communities involve extended ties since birth between individuals, in addition to their participation in common institutions. In Mathare, in contrast, although some of the inhabitants, particularly the leaders, had known each other prior to their moving into the community, the network of ties was nowhere near as complete as it would be in a traditional community. The Kikuyu in Mathare 2 come from a wide range of rural communities, and in the majority of cases they have lived in other parts of the city before coming to Mathare. Second, there are other parts of the city, such as Bahati, where the percentage of Kikuyu is at the same high level as in Mathare, and where similar institutions are absent. Third, there are certainly parallels between the Mathare institutions and traditional Kikuyu ones, such as the similarity between the committee of elders and the Kikuyu clan elders (Lambert 1956; Middleton and Kershaw 1953), and the fact that the leaders are significantly older than the majority of the population. However, it is hard to identify such general principles as being distinctly Kikuyu, since virtually all the prominent tribes in Kenya traditionally had similar groups involved in dispute settlement and leadership. Finally, in Mathare there is the absence of age sets and age grades as well as the kinship basis of social and political organization, both of which were particularly prominent features of traditional Kikuyu society.

Level of isolation or autonomy

Urban neighborhoods are less isolated and autonomous than small rural communities.[3] Autonomy is, however, a continuous rather than a dichotomous variable, and there can be a good deal of variation among urban communities. In many neighborhoods which lack community-wide political institutions, there are often many strong social institutions that can have political relevance. Whyte (1966) shows that friendship groups, for example, formed on the basis of age, sex, and aspirations, can

3. Lee (1968) describes a fascinating effort to determine neighborhood boundaries from the point of view of individuals in an area. He finds a great deal of variation in viewpoints, and suggests that the urban neighborhood has different meanings to different people, which poses difficulties in assuming that all residents want or receive the same need fulfillment from a given neighborhood.

be mobilized for political activity from time to time. A recent study by Suttles (1968) of an ethnically-mixed nieghborhood in Chicago also shows the strength of social institutions in an area lacking community-wide political organization. In Stanleyville, Africans are involved in complex social networks based more on kinship and urban friendships than on location (Pons 1969).

In contrast, highly autonomous communities, especially those found in rural areas, often have relatively well-defined, formalized political institutions. Redfield (1930) not only notes the existence of community-wide institutions in his village study in Tepoztlán, but also stresses the high level of order and integration, partially attributable to the community's isolation. In a later comparative study, considering four villages in Yucatan at varying degrees of isolation from urban centers, he concluded that loss of isolation and increasing heterogeneity are associated with increasing social disintegration (Redfield 1947:307). Thus we expect that the higher the isolation, the more likely an area is to be politically integrated.

In Nairobi, where there are few traditional neighborhoods and where housing pressures are severe, few people feel that neighborhoods are meaningful social or political communities. In Mathare, in contrast, social conditions have made the community more isolated and distinct than most. Nonetheless, its isolation is high only in relation to other parts of the city, and is probably more psychological than social. Most people leave the community every day, even if they do not work outside the area.

The isolation of Mathare 2 is hardly high in terms of its integration into the social and political life in the wider society. Most important, the continued success of the beer business is dependent on the outsiders who come to purchase the beer. Government officials, administrators, and the police are frequently in the community, and their presence provides more evidence of Mathare's lack of autonomy or isolation from the wider society. Kiboro and other leaders are quite involved in

TABLE 9.1 SUMMARY OF VARIABLES EXPLAINING LOCAL-LEVEL INTEGRATION IN MATHARE 2

Variable	Indicator	Score
Small size, face-to-face interactions	Population (approximately 2,000)	Low / medium
	Face-to-face versus mediated interactions	High
Level of isolation or autonomy	Economic independence from wider society (e.g., beer business, small business)	Low / medium
	Absence of government officials, administrators, and police in the community	Low
	Lack of involvement of community leaders in city politics	Low
	Absence of children from Mathare in city schools	Medium
	Lack of social services provided by government	High
	Government classification of Mathare as illegal	High

city politics in Nairobi, and are prominent in the organization of the local Member of Parliament, Dr. Waiyaki. Children from Mathare attend government schools throughout the city, although the attendance rates are not as high as those from other neighborhoods. At the same time, the lack of integration of Mathare into the broader community is seen in the lack of social services and in the official government policy of nonrecognition of the illegal community.

Conclusions

Political integration in Mathare 2 is partially affected by the fact that it is a small local community in which interactions are typically unmediated and by the fact that it has a moderate level of isolation from the wider society, as summarized in Table 9.1. Its small size and face-to-face interactions increase the visibility of local leaders, institutions, and problems, and hasten the outcomes of the integration process, whether they are successful or not. Its moderate level of isolation serves to make it more integrated than most nonisolated communities.

Eleven different independent variables have been introduced in attempting to explain the level of political integration found in Mathare 2 at the time of this study. The next important question to consider is their relative importance in understanding Mathare's integration, and the ways in which they are interrelated.

10

The political
integration of
urban squatters

Mathare 2 and the concept of community

Mathare 2 is clearly a community in that it possesses the
four characteristics of community outlined earlier, at least at
a minimal level. There is a particular geographic area associated
with Mathare 2, although some of the boundaries are less clearly
marked than others. The people living in Mathare 2 also identify
it as politically and socially distinct. For some people the most
relevant distinction is between Mathare 2 and the other villages
in the area, while for a much smaller group Mathare is part
of Nairobi, which is distinct from the rural areas. Thus Mathare
2 is neither maximally nor minimally distinct from other communities. Third, there is a more or less regular and identifiable
pattern of social relations and institutions found in Mathare 2.
Although the community's institutions do not work perfectly,
and there could undoubtedly be more and stronger ones, they
clearly operate in a regular and identifiable manner. Finally,
the organization of the territory is not based on a single goal.
There are a number of institutions and practices in the area
and it is hard to ascribe to them a single purpose, such as could
be done in the case of a corporation.

As an urban community, Mathare is not the only one in

which its residents regularly participate. Even though most people do not have jobs outside Mathare, they do leave the village. They make trips to various markets, attend religious institutions, and visit friends in other parts of the city. Thus in some ways an urban community such as Mathare can never be as important to its members as a rural one, which many people may leave only a few times in their entire lives.

The issue of whether "real" communities exist any more is a spurious one in many ways. In some cases skeptics base their theories on false conceptions of the degree of isolation in traditional rural communities. Despite arguments to the contrary, it must also be recognized that the absence of autonomy does not necessarily mean the absence of community. Other variables are also involved.

After studying the new suburban community of Levittown, New Jersey, Gans concludes that while sense of community and community institutions in Levittown were not well developed, living there did require people to act in community roles in at least certain areas of life (1967:146). He contends that Levittown was not a community by "traditional criteria" in that it was

> not an economic unit whose members were dependent on each other for their livelihood, and it was not a social unit for there was no reason or incentive for people to relate to each other as Levittowners on any regular basis. And Levittown was clearly not a symbolic unit, for the sense of community was weak. (1967:145)

Nonetheless, Gans was able to write some 433 pages about the "ways of life and politics in a new suburban community" in which he details often complex patterns of social and political organization found there. He outlines the ways in which the residents moving into a newly built suburb begin to form voluntary associations and political parties, and to interact with one another on a selective basis. Levittown is not the only community

191

in which they participate in their daily lives, but it certainly is a community.

What is probably needed is more attention to what *is* happening rather than to what *is not* happening in communities such as Mathare 2 or Levittown. Gans's detailed description of the community's institutions and values shows the ways in which this local community is and is not important in people's lives. At the same time modern technology has changed the space-time ratio so drastically that geographical constraints on individual social and political action *appear* to be much weaker than in the past. What is needed is empirical work aimed at determining to what extent this is actually true. The study of community formation in Mathare 2 can serve as a basis for developing a more rigorous conceptualization of the ways in which community values and institutions are shaped.

Political integration in Mathare 2

Mathare Valley Village 2 is a relatively well-integrated political community in which residents share a sense of community and a set of community-wide political institutions which help to provide orderly management and peaceful resolutions of political and social problems. The task now is to assess the relative importance of the previously discussed independent variables in explaining the level of political integration present in Mathare 2. Table 10.1 shows that while each of the independent variables is judged to have contributed to the over-all level of political integration, certain ones seem to have been particularly prominent. Six variables are scored "high" in importance and deserve particular attention as major explanatory factors.[1]

1. The high, medium, and low scores for each variable are composite judgments by the author of the relative contribution of each variable to the political integration of the community. This procedure of assigning scores to estimate the relative importance of each independent variable is selected because of the inability to use any other, possibly more intersubjectively verifiable, method in this situation.

TABLE 10.1 RELATIVE IMPORTANCE OF VARIABLES ACCOUNTING FOR
POLITICAL INTEGRATION IN MATHARE 2

Variable	Relative Importance in Explaining Integration
Independent variables primarily influencing sense of community:	
1. Perceived importance of community in the lives of the participants	High
2. Threats to participation and membership in the community	High
3. Existence of community symbols	Low
4. Participation in community activities and rituals	Medium
Independent variables primarily influencing institutional strength:	
5. Social and cultural homogeneity (a distinctive way of life)	High
6. Level of interactions internal to the community (mutual relevance)	Medium
7. Mutual interdependence	Medium
8. Institutional generalizability (spillover)	High
9. Skills of leaders	High
Independent variables influencing integration in a local community:	
10. Degree of isolation	Low/medium
11. Degree to which the community is small and interactions are unmediated and of a face-to-face nature	High

Perceived importance of the community

Unlike people living in most other neighborhoods in the city of Nairobi, more of the residents of Mathare are tied to their community for their livelihood. Individuals working in the southern industrial area or the central city prefer to live as close as possible to their jobs, but they do not have to do so. In addition, with a job and steady income, they can afford the rents charged in City Council–sponsored and private housing. Mathare residents lack these options. The location of their community is of crucial importance to the majority of residents engaged in the quasi-legal economy based on beer brewing and prostitution. Furthermore, the community is important to participants because it represents a way of cutting expenditures to the bare minimum. The residents of Mathare have few social alternatives. Most do not have jobs which would provide them with the economic alternative of living elsewhere, nor do they have access to the resources which would permit them to leave the urban areas altogether.

The result is that they perceive the community of Mathare 2 as important in their lives. They begin to develop a sense of common fate, a belief that their welfare is linked to that of their neighbors and of the community in general. This helps to explain the high level of compliance with community decisions, such as almost universal payment of local voluntary taxes in an area where there is, at the same time, widespread nonpayment of authorized Kenya government taxes.

Threats to participation and membership in the community

Just as the presence of external enemies can help to unify divided nations, external hostility is effective in uniting urban squatters. In Latin America, local organization is strongest and most effective when governments are highly vocal about moving squatters off illegally seized land. When the level of threat gets so high that squatters feel they have no chance of success, however, their unity collapses. Conversely, as communities become better established and begin to receive governmental services, the threat to tenure diminishes, and community organization usually weakens. Thus threat is curvilinearly related to integration, having its most positive effect when threat is high, but not so high that squatters cannot cope with it.

In Mathare the major external threat is not the possibility

of eviction; it is continual police action against the major source of income in the community—beer brewing. This threat is continually present in the form of police raids and of policemen who solicit bribes and favors in the community, and is a major impetus for both community organization and community cooperation in beer production and distribution.

External threat moved residents toward increased cooperation and also increased their perception of interdependence, as they developed a sense of the ways in which they are distinct from the rest of the population of the city. The negative image of Mathare held by the wider society, including many government officials, further served to separate Mathare residents from other people in the city.

Social and cultural homogeneity

Life in Mathare 2 is distinctive in a number of ways. Most noticeable is the marginal subsistence economy based on beer brewing. A second distinction is the social homogeneity of the population. Almost everyone is equally poor and unskilled, in comparison with the wider population of the city. The residents are mainly Kikuyu, and many share common memories and experiences from the 1950s, when they spent time in detention. Others who were just children at the time recall the dislocation, the loss of relatives, and the social insecurity that typified the era. In more recent times, this ethnic identity has been transformed into support for KANU and President Kenyatta.

The distinctive way of life of these urban Kikuyu squatters is important in the integration process in two ways. It helps provide a common bond between individuals, stressing shared past experiences and events that build a collective identity, and it contributes to common understandings and perceptions important in the daily operation of community institutions. The existence of other areas in the city which are equally homogeneous but less well integrated shows that this variable is hardly a sufficient condition for political integration. Nonetheless, it does seem to be a necessary condition in that people must come to perceive themselves as sharing a distinctive life style before integration can proceed.

Institutional generalizability

The village leaders in Mathare are quite successful in expanding the tasks of existing organizations and in creating new organizations as problems arise. Task expansion and spillover of political institutions are crucial in the integration process. Integration cannot increase in communities where the scope of operation of the existing institutions is strictly limited; it requires task expansion through organizations whose functions are not too narrowly defined. Rapid task expansion such as occurred in Mathare 2 is partially dependent on the successful completion of previous tasks. Successful organizations grow; unsuccessful ones do not. Success, in this context, is measured by the perception of the residents of the community, rather than along an objective scale of external judgment.

Leadership skills

Probably the most important variable accounting for the level of political integration in Mathare 2 is the nature of leadership skills available in the community. In particular, the perceived effectiveness of the leaders in the community is high; also, the leaders are particularly aggressive in seeking task expansion and broader powers for existing institutions. The major difference between Mathare 2 and the other villages in the area, where community organizations were less successful, is that the leaders of the other villages were less skilled.

While Kiboro, as the village head, is a highly effective leader and an extremely colorful individual, leadership in Mathare is not a one-man affair. Others often put in a great deal of time on projects that Kiboro started but which he could not complete alone. For example, Kiboro might tell the elders to hear a particular case; Kinami, the assistant secretary, would have it recorded; and Kariuki would call together the elders, who would spend several hours listening to both sides and making a decision. Gitau, the secretary, spends many hours typing the minutes of village meetings, writing letters for individuals in the community, and keeping the records for the cooperative society and the social hall.

One reason the leadership is successful is because of its honesty in situations where most people would expect it to be dishonest. Kiboro for the most part seeks power and prestige, rather than material gain, through his leadership position. The leaders are careful in handling money collected from the public. Generally they place public funds in a bank account that requires three or four signatures for a withdrawal.

The importance of Kiboro's leadership is shown in several accounts of village events following his arrest and subsequent acquittal in 1969, after this study had been completed. At that time he was in prison for nine months. The remaining leaders tried to continue to run the community as Kiboro had, but the youth wing intervened with a *coup d'état*, ordering the older leaders to leave the village office and to give up their keys. They remained in power for several months, extracting bribes and tricking community residents, and were forced to flee the community only when Kiboro was released from prison and the old system reinstated.

Small, face-to-face community

The last important variable accounting for the high level of political integration in Mathare is the small size of the community, in which most interactions are face to face. Feedback is rapid, and both individuals and institutions are highly visible. This, combined with the aggressive leadership described above, creates the integrative process which many functionalists describe. An active leadership promotes the task expansion of existing institutions and the development of new organizations in the community. Reinforcement is strong, as the entire community is often aware of the leaders' activities within a short period of time in a village such as Mathare.

Because of these conditions, it is expected that the integration process, whether successful or unsuccessful, should be more rapid on the local level than on the international one, as long as local conditions promote rapid feedback and a mutual salience between actors. High visibility is not always a good thing, however. If leaders quickly get credit for their sucesses, they are chastised with equal speed when they fail. A new organization sometimes will do well to operate out of the limelight until it gains some experience. Probably one of the greatest problems for the United Nations was that it was the most visible international organization in the world, and people came to expect certain unrealistic results from it in areas where it had no power to act. Today its prestige has diminished, although it is still active in many areas and probably operates with a much more realistic idea of what is possible than it did initially.

Hypothesized phases in the community formation process

An alternative to considering the independent variables affecting the level of integration one at a time, or to searching for a single variable which best explains integration, is to hypothesize a pattern of relationships among the variables. The advantage of this procedure is that it permits a consideration of complex relationships between several variables at a time, as well as speculation concerning the order in which the variables are relevant in the integration process. Figure 10.1 arranges the eleven independent variables into three groups representing different phases of the community formation process in Mathare

FIGURE 10.1 HYPOTHESIZED PHASES IN THE COMMUNITY FORMATION PROCESS IN MATHARE 2

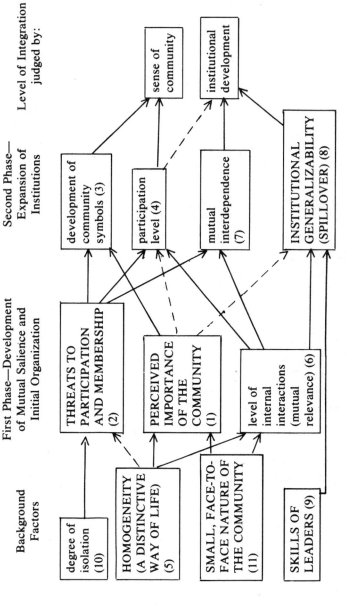

CAPITALS indicate variables judged high in their contribution to integration in Mathare 2.
Numbers in parentheses coincide with the number of each variable in Table 10.1, above.

———— strong link
— — — moderate link

Background Factors

First Phase—Development of Mutual Salience and Initial Organization

Second Phase— Expansion of Institutions

Level of Integration judged by:

degree of isolation (10)

HOMOGENEITY (A DISTINCTIVE WAY OF LIFE) (5)

SMALL, FACE-TO-FACE NATURE OF THE COMMUNITY (11)

SKILLS OF LEADERS (9)

THREATS TO PARTICIPATION AND MEMBERSHIP (2)

PERCEIVED IMPORTANCE OF THE COMMUNITY (1)

level of internal interactions (mutual relevance) (6)

development of community symbols (3)

participation level (4)

mutual interdependence (7)

INSTITUTIONAL GENERALIZABILITY (SPILLOVER) (8)

sense of community

institutional development

2. It is hoped that stating these relationships in relatively general terms will make possible systematic testing of our hypotheses in local, national, and international communities.

Background factors

The first group of four variables represents background factors, or fixed inputs over which the members of the community as well as of the wider society have little control. For example, Mathare 2 has a relatively high level of social and cultural homogeneity. Short of the forced movement of people from other parts of the city into the village and the eviction of present residents, there is little that can be done to change this condition.

The background factors do not promote a given level of political integration directly; rather, they operate to affect other conditions in the community formation process. In Mathare 2, as is shown in Figure 10.1, the degree of isolation (10)—the fact that Mathare is a small neighborhood in the larger urban system— is the most important determinant of the level of outside threat (2) directed at the community, while the distinctiveness or homogeneity (5) of the community also makes the community vulnerable to threat.[2] Homogeneity similarly contributes to increasing the perceived importance of the community in people's lives (1), and to the relatively high level of interactions within the community (6) as compared with other neighborhoods of the city. The third background condition, the small, face-to-face nature of the community (11), explains the development of the perceived importance of the community in people's lives (1) as well as high levels of interaction within Mathare 2 (6). Finally, the skills of the leaders (9) are considered a crucial background condition in developing the feelings of institutional generalizability (8).

2. The numbers in parentheses represent the number of each variable in Table 10.1.

First phase—development of mutual salience and initial organization

The first phase in the community formation process is the development of mutual awareness or salience among the community participants as initial organization is achieved. Residents in Mathare became aware that other members of the community had problems similar to their own and that their solutions were, at least in part, linked. The earliest organizational efforts in Mathare did not seek a solution uniquely concerned with the community, but were channeled through KANU and aimed at achieving national political independence and a change in values of the government vis-à-vis squatters.

During this phase the crucial variables are the level of outside threat, the perceived importance of the community in the lives of the participants, and the pattern of interactions in Mathare. Each of these is related to different background factors and in turn will determine in part the subsequent stages in the community formation process. In trying to determine whether community consciousness preceded institutional development in Mathare, the data appear to indicate that the two began and grew together.

Accounts from older residents indicate that a great deal of the early sense of community in Mathare was attributable to the fact that many of the early residents had lived in Mathare prior to the Emergency, and that a sense of solidarity developed among them due to common Emergency experiences. As organizational efforts directed toward national politics proved successful and KANU became Kenya's ruling party, sense of community increased with the recognition of Mathare by politicians and the establishment of the nursery school and local village committees. Thus in the functionalist-interactionist debate about whether community institutions or sense of community should come first, the answer from Mathare is that the two grow almost simultaneously, with small changes in one being related to small changes in the other.

Returning to the relationships outlined in Figure 10.1, the level of threat (2) is seen as contributing to the development of mutual interdependence within the community (7), the development of community symbols (3), and the level of participation in community institutions and rituals (4). The perceived importance of the community (1) helps explain the development of community symbols (3), as well as increasing participation (4) and institutional generalizability (8). Increasing interactions within the community (6) raise the level of participation (4), the level of mutual interdependence (7), and the institutional generalizability (8).

Second phase—expansion of institutions

The second phase in the process of community formation in Mathare stressed the expansion of existing institutions and the growth of new community organizations. In particular, this phase can be identified with the building of the social hall, the establishment of the cooperative, the installation of the water supply, and the expansion of the nursery school. It is during this period that leadership skills are particularly important in determining the course of institutional growth; poor leaders can destroy weak institutions, while good leaders improve them.

Institutional growth requires expansion of capabilities and the presentation to community institutions of demands which are solvable with existing resources. When demands can be met, further expansion is possible and feelings of community consciousness can increase; if the demands require resources beyond local means, institutions can stagnate and eventually fail. In Mathare most of the problems presented to local leaders proved to be solvable—the regulation of beer brewing in the social hall, the establishment of the nursery school, and the installation of a water supply, for example. At the same time, the leaders attempted to work toward the solution of two more serious problems—jobs and permanent land tenure. People in the community had a relatively realistic sense of what problems the local institutions and leaders could solve and which ones they could not. As a result, political institutions in Mathare were not burdened with demands whose solutions were beyond the capacities of the local leaders.

As is shown in Figure 10.1, the development of community symbols (3) and the participation level (4) directly affect the sense of community, while institutional development is a function of mutual interdependence (7), institutional generalizability (8), and participation level (4).

Additional phases in the community formation process

At the conclusion of the study of Mathare 2 in 1968 the community appeared to have finished the second phase of the community formation process. The sense of community was relatively strong and a wide range of community institutions were operating in a number of areas. At the same time, several questions can be raised about the future development of political organizations in Mathare in particular and about the political integration process in squatter communities in general.

The greatest weakness of local organizations in Mathare from their inception has been their inability to deal successfully with the two most pressing problems that face urban squatters in Nairobi—jobs and housing security. At times the community has sought to do something about each of these problems, but limited resources in these and several other areas create limits on local organizational efforts. Through the operation of the social hall and through contacts with local political officials and businessmen, the community has arranged subsistence employment or occasional work for some residents, but not for nearly as many as needed it. However, the major strategy in the job area was to provide an atmosphere where people could support themselves through beer brewing, petty commerce, or renting rooms. By 1969, with encouragement and assistance from the

National Christian Council of Kenya (NCCK), a program of small cottage industry, such as shirt-making, was started in the village. However, the number of individuals involved and the profits the program earned were minuscule in comparison with the need.

The problem of securing permanent land tenure either in the village or elsewhere is a second problem village leaders have sought in vain to solve. In the independence period, many Mathare residents, being landless, hoped that they could obtain a *shamba* (farm) in one of the settlement schemes in the former White Highlands, which they heard were being given to landless Africans, and particularly to Kikuyu. Unfortunately, there was relatively little land to be had, political connections were often needed to secure any, and, most important, it was not free and required sizable initial and monthly payments. Thus only a handful of urban squatters obtained land in the rural areas.

Realizing that this was not the answer to the land security problem, village leaders decided to raise money in the community in order to purchase a plot of land near Nairobi where they would no longer be squatters. This was part of the reason for the establishment of the cooperative society and the social hall. The leaders hoped that sufficient capital could be raised through these institutions to make a sizable payment on such a plot. By 1966 they found a piece of land for sale in eastern Nairobi, south of Kariobangi, and agreed to the seller's price. They reported that they were unable to purchase the land, however, as the government considered the price too high and did not allow the sale. By 1968 and 1969 a number of land-buying cooperatives were formed, with the idea of buying land in the Mathare Valley area. Most of the capital came from outsiders, and changes in land ownership and the construction of new houses on the plot that was purchased had little effect on the squatters, other than raising the population density of the general area.

Another important limitation of the local institutions is their inability to undertake necessary community projects requiring large capital investments. While the community was able eventually to raise the funds and hire the plumbers needed to run one water line to the center of the village, there is a need for many more water supply points. As the population density increases, the need for the construction of sewers and permanent latrines also becomes more pressing. These sorts of expenditures are beyond the means of the community at present, and can only be made through government involvement in Mathare.

At the same time, government initiative in these areas, although desperately needed, will probably have the effect of weakening local organization and leadership, as it has in squatter communities in Latin America. It is hardly likely that the government will channel assistance through the local leadership, thus strengthening its power base. This means that as the Nairobi and Kenya governments move toward recognizing the rights of Mathare's squatters and helping to improve their living conditions, there is the probability that local organization, which was created in part as a defense against outside threats, will be weakened.

The last question to be raised in analyzing the community formation process is the "second-generation problem." In his study of an Israeli kibbutz, Spiro (1963) noted many differences between the generation that established the community and their children. Parallel differences can be observed in urban squatter communities such as Mathare, and these should have important effects on the kind of community Mathare will be in fifteen years.

Most adults living in Mathare have low expectations about the possibility of great changes taking place during their lives, but at the same time they have high aspirations for their children. One reason that the community leadership has been so effective is its educational efforts—the establishment of the village school for the younger children and Kiboro's success in getting children into Kenya government schools, often with part- or full-tuition scholarships. Despite the greater education of the younger generation in Mathare, it is probable that many, if not most, will be unable to find regular jobs when they finish school, as available jobs are increasing only slowly in comparison with the number of job seekers in Kenya. Whether these young people will be content with the same quasi-legal status as their parents is impossible to say at present. It seems reasonable, however, to expect that there may be different organizational responses from the second generation of urban squatters than from the first.

Urban squatters in world perspective

Squatters constitute an important proportion of the uban population in the world. Although they are found in greater numbers in Africa, Asia, and Latin America, there are also squatters in European cities such as Paris and Rome. Just like their counterparts in the developing world, squatters in Europe are looking for ways to reduce expenses and at the same time to increase their control over their daily lives. In short, the squatter phenomenon is likely to be neither temporary nor insignificant. Instead, as Turner points out, it is part of the response to the unprecedented urban growth rates of the present century.

Although squatting as a distinct phenomenon can be isolated in many diverse cities, it can take different forms, produce different reactions from government and the wider society, and go through different stages. Turner hypothesizes that differences between provisional, incipient, and status-seeker communities are a function of the age of the settlement and the wealth of the residents. His data are cross-sectional; that is, he looked at three communities at one point in time, rather than at one or more communities across time. At present, however, there are not enough data available to permit very sophisticated analyses of these differences. Even in Latin America, where squatting has been studied most extensively, available data are still limited. In Africa and Asia, information is scattered and minimal. The applicability to other areas of the world of typologies or developmental cycles proposed for Latin American settlements is as yet undetermined. If the processes of urbanization follow a similar pattern in all three areas, it would be expected that the experiences of Latin American squatters would also have strong parallels in other areas in future decades, particularly in Africa. If, on the other hand, the differences in the urbanizing experiences of the three areas are more important than the similarities, the squatting experiences may also be highly divergent.

Mathare 2 is a better organized and more integrated community than Turner's or Mangin's hypotheses would lead one to expect. At the same time, the changes in the developmental cycle appear to be taking place at a slower rate in Mathare than they would expect to find on the basis of the Latin American experience. Exactly why this is so is not clear.

Turner expects that the greater the proportion of the population that is employed, the more permanent a community will be, and the more likely the government will be to grant recognition and assistance to the settlement. This had not taken place in Mathare by the end of the study. The marginal economy of Mathare Valley, based on beer brewing, set a firm upper limit on the capital available to local residents for the physical improvement of their houses. While most people now have metal roofs and thicker walls than before, there is no movement toward building with more permanent materials—cement, stone, brick, or wood—such as has taken place in Kariobangi, the nearby site-and-service scheme.

A second reason for the lack of physical improvements is the uncertain status of the community. The government has refused to officially recognize the rights of the Mathare squatters to the land they reside on, and has ordered a limit to the number and kind of buildings in the area. In addition, the growth of land-buying cooperatives which purchase land in the Mathare area has led to conflicts between present squatters and new landlords who wish to build houses on their recently acquired land. Reportedly squatters from one village in Mathare were part of a cooperative purchasing occupied land in another Mathare village. Instead of being relatively sympathetic with the squatters' plight, the new owners took a firm position in trying to evict them from their land.

The uncertain status of Mathare, and probably of any other squatter community, is demoralizing to the residents and has an adverse effect on self-help and improvement schemes. Governmental recognition and the provision of certain improvements, such as a road and permanent latrines in the area, could provide a better life for the people in Mathare in the most humane and least expensive manner possible. The pleading of government officials for the squatters to return to the land is a hopeless course of action, as they have no land to which they can return. On the other hand, governmental promises to build permanent housing for everyone needing it are just as unrealistic, because not even a fraction of the capital necessary for such a plan is available.

As the government begins to change its attitudes toward Mathare, it needs to recognize the importance of local institutions and leaders in any plans that it develops. Admittedly this will be extremely difficult, both because of the paternalistic values of government officials and administrators and because of their fear of adding to the power of local leaders. If it is channeled through local institutions, however, governmental assistance can take advantage of local initiative and resources, which would both cut costs and teach people the ways in which they can better their own lives in the city.

This, of course, is often difficult for educated government officials to accept. In developing countries where the government officials are often highly educated in comparison with the people they serve, and where democratic values were not an important part of the colonial system, paternalism is a pose frequently assumed by the bureaucracy toward the public. One day in Mathare, an official of the Ministry of Cooperatives and Social Services visited the community to look at the records for the cooperative. Because Gitau was quite conscientious and had attended a special Cooperative College course, the books were in good order. The official studied them for about twenty mintues and then turned to Gitau, Kiboro, and other villagers, all of whom were somewhat meek and humble in his presence, and told them the books were not fully acceptable because Gitau had "failed to skip a line between entries in the minutes of the meetings." Then there was a short discussion about how this was to be corrected, and at one point it was suggested that they might recopy all of the minutes in the correct manner. Instead of being pleased that there were any records at all, and praising the care and accuracy with which they had been kept, this official chose to find some basis for criticism of the community leaders in order to justify his superior status.

In squatter communities, local organization is generally weak and the capabilities of local institutions limited. To the extent that Mathare 2 is a partial exception, it can help in developing an understanding of the variables which are most important in the political integration process. While a single case study can prove little in itself, it may serve the purpose of generating hypotheses that can subsequently be examined in various settings. In this way the first step toward successful organization made by squatters in Mathare 2 may increase our understanding of the ways in which community is created in a wide range of social and cultural contexts.

Bibliography

ABRAMS, CHARLES
1964 *Man's Struggle for Shelter in an Urbanizing World.*
Cambridge: MIT Press.
1965 "Squatter Settlements: The Problem and the Opportunity." Washington, D.C.: Department of Housing and Urban Development.

ALMOND, GABRIEL, AND SIDNEY VERBA
1963 *The Civic Culture.* Princeton, N.J.: Princeton University Press.

ARCINAS, FE RODRIGUEZ
1955 "A Socio Economic Study of Manila Squatters," *The Philippine Sociological Review,* III (January), 35-41.

BALES, ROBERT F.
1950 "A Set of Categories for the Analysis of Small Group Interaction," *American Sociological Review,* XV (April), 257-63.

BASCOM, WILLIAM
1955 "Urbanization among the Yoruba," *American Journal of Sociology,* LX, no. 5, 446-54.

BECKER, HOWARD
1963 *The Outsiders.* New York: Free Press.

BENNETT, GEORGE
1963 *Kenya: A Political History, the Colonial Period.* London: Oxford University Press.

BEYER, GLENN, ED.
1967 *The Urban Explosion in Latin America.* Ithaca, N.Y.: Cornell University Press.

BOGUE, DONALD J., AND K. C. ZACHARIAH
1962 "Urbanization in India: Past and Future." In *India's*

210

Urban Future, edited by Roy Turner. Berkeley and Los Angeles: University of California Press.

BONILLA, FRANK
1970 "Rio's Favelas: The Rural Slum Within the City." In *Peasants in Cities,* edited by William Maugin. Boston: Houghton Mifflin.

BOSE, ASHISH
1971 "The Urbanization Process in South and Southeast Asia." In *Urbanization and National Development,* edited by Leo Jakobson and Ved Prakash, pp. 81-109. Vol. I. South and Southeast Asia Urban Affairs Annals. Beverly Hills: Sage Publications.

BREESE, GERALD
1966 *Urbanization in Newly Developing Countries.* Englewood Cliffs, N.J.: Prentice-Hall.

BREESE, GERALD, ED.
1969 *The City in Newly Developing Countries.* Englewood Cliffs, N.J.: Prentice-Hall.

BROWNING, HARLEY L.
1967 "Urbanization and Modernization in Latin America: The Demographic Perspective." In *The Urban Explosion in Latin America,* edited by Glenn Beyer. Ithaca, N.Y.: Cornell University Press.

CAMPBELL, ANGUS, ET AL.
1960 *The American Voter.* New York: John Wiley.

CAPLOW, THEODORE, SHELDON STRYKER, AND SAMUEL E. WALLACE
1964 *The Urban Ambience.* Totowa, N.J.: Bedminster Press.

CHAMBERS, ROBERT
1969 *Settlement Schemes in Tropical Africa.* London: Routledge and Kegan Paul.

COBB, ROGER W., AND CHARLES ELDER
1969 *International Community.* New York: Holt, Rinehart and Winston.
1972 "Individual Orientations in the Study of Political Symbolism," *Social Science Quarterly.* LIII (June), 79-90.

CORNELIUS, WAYNE, JR.

1969 "Urbanization as an Agent in Latin American Political Instability: The Case of Mexico," *American Political Science Review*, LXIII (Spring), 833–57.

1971 "The Political Sociology of Cityward Migration in Latin America: Toward Empirical Theory." In *Latin American Urban Research*, edited by Francine F. Rabinovitz and Felicity M. Trueblood. Vol I. Beverly Hills: Sage Publications.

COSER, LOUIS

1956 *The Functions of Social Conflict.* New York: Free Press.

DANIELSKI, DAVID J.

1961 "The Influence of the Chief Justice in the Decisional Process." In *Courts, Judges and Politics*, edited by Walter F. Murphy and C. Herman Pritchett. New York: Random House.

DAVIS, KINGSLEY

1962 "Urbanization in India: Past and Future." In *India's Urban Future*, edited by Roy Turner. Berkeley and Los Angeles: University of California Press.

1968 "The Urbanization of the Human Population." In *Urbanism in World Perspective*, edited by Sylvia Fleis Fava. New York: Thomas Y. Crowell.

1969 *World Urbanization 1950–1970. Vol. I. Basic Data for Cities, Countries, and Regions.* Population Monograph Series, no. 4, University of California. Berkeley: Institute of International Studies.

DAVIS, KINGSLEY, AND ANA CASIS

1957 "Urbanization in Latin America." In *Cities and Society*, edited by Paul K. Hatt and Albert J. Reiss, Jr. New York: Free Press.

DEUTSCH, KARL

1964 "Communication Theory and Political Integration." In *The Integration of Political Communities: An Anthology*, edited by Philip Jacob and James Toscano. Philadelphia: Lippincott.

DEUTSCH, KARL, ET AL.
1957 *Political Community and the North Atlantic Area.*
Princeton, N.J.: Princeton University Press.
1966 "Political Community and the North Atlantic Area."
In *International Political Communities: An Anthology.*
Garden City, N.Y.: Doubleday Anchor Books.

DIETZ, HENRY
1969 "Urban Squatter Settlements in Peru: A Case History
and Analysis," *Journal of Inter-American Studies,* XI,
no. 3 (July), 353-70.

DOUGHTY, PAUL L.
1970 "Behind the Back of the City: 'Provincial' Life in Lima,
Peru." In *Peasants in Cities,* edited by William P. Mangin. Boston: Houghton Mifflin.

DWYER, D. J.
1964 "The Problem of In-Migration and Squatter Settlement
in Asian Cities: Two Case Studies, Manila and Victoria-
Kowloon," *Asian Studies,* II, no. 2, 145-69.

EASTON, DAVID
1964 *A Systems Analysis of Political Life.* New York: John
Wiley.

EDELMAN, MURRAY
1964 *The Symbolic Uses of Politics.* Urbana: University of
Illinois Press.
1971 *Politics as Symbolic Action.* Chicago: Markham.

EPSTEIN, A. L.
1958 *Politics in an Urban African Community.* Manchester:
Manchester University Press.

EVANS-PRITCHARD, E. E.
1968 *The Nuer.* London: Oxford University Press.

FALLERS, LLOYD
1955 "The Predicament of the Modern African Chief,"
American Anthropologist, LVII (April), 290-305.

FORRESTER, MARION
1962 *Kenya Today: Social Prerequisites for Economic Development.* The Hague: Mouton.

213

FRANKENBERG, RONALD
1966 *Communities in Britain.* Middlesex: Penguin Books.

GANS, HERBERT
1967 *The Levittowners.* New York: Vintage Books.

GERMANI, GINO
1961 "Inquiry into the Social Effects of Urbanization in a Working-Class Sector of Greater Buenos Aires." In *Urbanization in Latin America,* edited by Philip Hauser. New York: International Documents Service, Columbia University Press.

GIBBS, JAMES
1963 "The Kpelle Moot," *Africa,* XXXIII, no. 1 (January), 1–10.

GIST, NOEL P.
1968 "Urbanization in India." In *Urbanism in World Perspective,* edited by Sylvia Fleis Fava. New York: Thomas Y. Crowell.

GLUCKMAN, MAX
1960 "Tribalism in Modern British Central Africa," *Cahiers d'études africaines,* I, no. 1, 55–70.
1966 *Custom and Politics in Africa.* Oxford: Basil Blackwell.

GOLDRICH, DANIEL
1970 "Political Organization and the Politicization of the Poblador," *Comparative Political Studies,* III, no. 2 (July), 176–202.

GOLDRICH, DANIEL, RAYMOND B. PRATT, AND C. R. SCHULLER
1967 "The Political Integration of Lower-Class Urban Settlements in Chile and Peru," *Studies in Comparative International Development,* Vol. III, no. 1.

GORDON, MILTON
1964 *Assimilation in American Life.* New York: Oxford University Press.

GREER, SCOTT
1962 *The Emerging City.* New York: John Wiley.

GREER, SCOTT, AND DAVID MINAR, EDS.
   1969. *The Concept of Community*. Chicago: Aldine.

GUETZKOW, HAROLD
   1955 *Multiple Loyalties: A Theoretical Approach to a Problem in International Organization*. Princeton, N.J.: Center for Research on World Political Institutions.

GUHA, UMA
   1958 *A Short Sample Survey of the Socio-Economic Conditions of Saheb-Bagan Bustee, Rajabazar, Calcutta*. Calcutta: The Pooran Press.

HAAS, ERNST
   1958 *The Uniting of Europe*. Stanford, Calif.: Stanford University Press.
   1964 *Beyond the Nation-State*. Stanford, Calif.: Stanford University Press.
   1965 "International Integration: The European and the Universal Process." In *International Political Communities: An Anthology*. Garden City, N.Y.: Doubleday Anchor Books.
   1970 "The Study of Regional Integration." In *Regional Integration: Theory and Research*, edited by Leon Lindberg and Stuart Scheingold. Cambridge: Harvard University Press.

HANCE, WILLIAM
   1970 *Population, Migration, and Urbanization in Africa*. New York: Columbia University Press.

HANNA, WILLIAM J., AND JUDITH L. HANNA
   1971 *Urban Dynamics in Black Africa*. Chicago: Aldine.

HARBESON, JOHN W.
   1971 "Land Reforms and Politics in Kenya, 1954-70," *Journal of Modern African Studies*, IX, no. 2, 231-51.

HELLMANN, ELLEN
   1969 *Rooiyard: A Sociological Survey of an Urban Native Slum Yard*. Rhodes-Livingston Papers, no. 13. Manchester: University of Manchester Press.

Bibliography

HERBERT, JOHN D., AND ALFRED P. VAN HUYCK, EDS.
1968 *Urban Planning in the Developing Countries.* New York: Praeger.

HILLERY, GEORGE A., JR.
1968 *Communal Organizations: A Study of Local Societies.* Chicago: University of Chicago Press.

HOMER, ELIZABETH L.
1971 "The Squatter Phenomenon: A Survey and Analysis." Unpublished paper. Bryn Mawr, Pa.: Bryn Mawr College, Department of Political Science.

HUNT, CHESTER, ET AL.
1963 *Sociology in the Philippine Setting.* Ovezone City: Phoenix Publishing House.

HYDEN, GORAN, ROBERT JACKSON, AND JOHN OKUMU, EDS.
1970 *Development Administration: The Kenyan Experience.* Nairobi: Oxford University Press.

JACOB, PHILIP, AND HENRY TEUNE
1964 "The Integrative Process: Guidelines for Analyses of the Bases of Political Integration." In *The Integration of Political Communities,* edited by Philip Jacob and James Toscano. Philadelphia: Lippincott.

JACOB, PHILIP, AND JAMES TOSCANO, EDS.
1964 *The Integration of Political Communities.* Philadelphia: Lippincott.

JOHNSON, WILLARD
1970 *The Cameroon Federation.* Princeton, N.J.: Princeton University Press.

KAYITENKORE, ETIENNE
1967 "La Construction dans les zones de squatting de Kinshasa," *Cahiers economiques et sociaux,* V (October), 327-54.

KELLER, SUZANNE
1968 *The Urban Neighborhood.* New York: Random House.

KENYA, GOVERNMENT OF
1964 *Population Census 1962.* Advance Report of Vols. I

and II (1964). Nairobi: Kenya Government Printer.

1966 *Population Census* 1962. Vol. II (1966). Nairobi: Kenya Government Printer.

1971 *Population Census* 1969. Vols. I–III. Nairobi: Kenya Government Printer.

KNOOP, HENRI

1966 "Some Demographic Characteristics of a Suburban Squatting Community of Leopoldville: A Preliminary Analysis," *Cahiers economiques et sociaux,* IV, no. 2 (June), 119–39.

1971 "The Sex Ratio of an African Squatter Settlement: An Exercise in Hypothesis Building," *African Urban Notes,* VI (Spring), 19–24.

KRAPF-ASKARI, EVA

1969 *Yoruba Towns and Cities.* Oxford: Clarendon Press.

LAMBERT, H. E.

1956 *Kikuyu Social and Political Institutions.* London: Oxford University Press.

LAQUIAN, A. A.

1964 "Isla de Ko Koma: Politics among Urban Slum Dwellers," *Philippine Journal of Public Administration,* Vol. VIII, no. 2 (April).

1971 "Slums and Squatters in South and Southeast Asia." In *Urbanization and National Development,* edited by Leo Jakobson and Ved Prakash, pp. 182–203. Vol. I. South and Southeast Asia Urban Affairs Annals. Beverly Hills: Sage Publications.

LEE, TERRENCE

1968 "Urban Neighborhood as a Socio-Spatial Schema," *Human Relations,* XXI, 241–67.

LEEDS, ANTHONY, AND ELIZABETH LEEDS

1970 "Brazil and the Myth of Urban Rurality: Urban Experience, Work, and Values in the 'Squatments' of Rio de Janeiro and Lima." In *City and Country in the Third World,* edited by Arthur J. Field. Cambridge, Mass.: Schenkman Publishing Co.

LEWIS, OSCAR
1965 "Urbanization without Breakdown." In *Contemporary Cultures and Societies of Latin America,* edited by Dwight B. Heath and Richard N. Adams, pp. 424-37. New York: Random House.

LEYS, COLIN
1971 "Politics in Kenya: The Development of Peasant Society," *British Journal of Political Science,* I, 307-37.

LINDBERG, LEON
1963 *The Dynamics of European Economic Integration.* Stanford, Calif.: Stanford University Press.

LINDBERG, LEON, AND STUART SCHEINGOLD, EDS.
1970 *Regional Integration: Theory and Practice.* Cambridge: Harvard University Press.

LITTLE, KENNETH
1965 *West African Urbanization.* New York: Cambridge Univeristy Press.

MCGEE, T. G.
1967 *The Southeast Asian City.* London: G. Bell and Sons.

MCVICAR, KENNETH G.
1969 "Twilight of an East African Slum: Pumwani and the Evolution of Settlement in Nairobi." Ph.D. dissertation, Department of Geography, UCLA.

MANGIN, WILLIAM P.
1965a "The Role of Regional Associations in the Adaptation of Rural Migrants to Cities in Peru." In *Contemporary Cultures and Societies of Latin America,* edited by Dwight B. Heath and Richard N. Adams. New York: Random House.

1965b "Mental Health and Migration to Cities: A Peruvian Case." In *Contemporary Cultures and Societies in Latin America,* edited by Dwight B. Heath and Richard N. Adams. New York: Random House.

1967 "Latin American Squatter Settlements: A Problem and a Solution," *Latin American Research Review,* II (Summer), 65-98.

1970 *Peasants in Cities: Readings in the Anthropology of Urbanization.* Boston: Houghton Mifflin.

MANGIN, WILLIAM P., AND JOHN C. TURNER
1968 "Benarides and the Barriada Movement," *Progressive Architecture* (May), pp. 154-62.

MAR, JOSE MATOS
1961 "The 'Barriadas' of Lima: An Example of Integration into Urban Life." In *Urbanization in Latin America,* edited by Philip Hauser. New York: International Documents Service, Columbia University Press, pp. 170-89.

MERRITT, RICHARD L.
1966 *Symbols of American Community, 1735-1765.* New Haven, Conn.: Yale University Press.

MIDDLETON, JOHN, AND GREET KERSHAW
1953 *The Kikuyu and Kamba of Kenya.* Ethnographic Survey of Africa. London: International African Institute.

MILBRATH, LESTER
1965 *Political Participation.* Chicago: Rand McNally.

MITRANY, DAVID
1966 *A Working Peace System.* Chicago: Quadrangle Books.

MORSE, RICHARD
1966 "Recent Research on Latin American Urbanization: A Selective Survey with Commentary," *Latin American Research Review,* I, 35-74.

NAIROBI CITY COUNCIL
1953 *Annual Report of the African Affairs Department, 1953.* Nairobi: Nairobi City Council.
1967 "City of Nairobi 1967 Planning Report #1: Population." Mimeographed. Nairobi: Nairobi City Council.

NAROLL, RAOUL
1962 *Data Quality Control.* New York: Free Press.

NELSON, JOAN
1969 *Migrants, Urban Poverty and Instability in Developing Nations.* Occasional Papers in International Affairs, no. 22. Cambridge, Mass.: Center for International Affairs.

NISBET, ROBERT
1962 *Community and Power*. New York: Oxford Galaxy Books.

NYE, JOSEPH S.
1970 "Comparing Common Markets: A Revised Neo-Functionalist Model." In *Regional Integration: Theory and Research*, edited by Leon Lindberg and Stuart Scheingold. Cambridge: Harvard University Press.
1971 *Peace in Parts*. Boston: Little, Brown.

PARKER, MARY
1949 *Political and Social Aspects of the Development of Municipal Government in Kenya with Special Reference to Nairobi*. London: Colonial Office.

PARKIN, DAVID
1969 *Neighbors and Nationals in an African City Ward*. Berkeley and Los Angeles: University of California Press.

PEARSE, ANDREW
1961 "Some Characteristics of Urbanization in the City of Rio de Janeiro." In *Urbanization in Latin America*, edited by Philip Hauser, pp. 191-205. New York: International Documents Service, Columbia University Press.

PERLMAN, JANICE ELAINE
1971 "The Fate of Migrants in Rio's Favelas: Portrait of the People." Paper presented to the Conference on Recent Research on Rural-Urban Migration at the American Academy of Arts and Sciences, Brookline, Massachusetts, November 19-21, 1971.

POLITICAL RECORD BOOK
1899 Kenya Government Archives. Nairobi.

PONS, VALDO
1969 *Stanleyville*. London: Oxford University Press.

PORTES, ALEJANDRO
1971 "The Urban Slum in Chile: Types and Correlates," *Land Economics*, XLVII, no. 3 (August), 235-48.

POWELL, SANDRA
1969 "Political Participation in the Barriadas: A Case Study," *Comparative Political Studies*, II, no. 2 (July), 195-215.

RAO, V. K. R. V., AND P. B. DESAI
1965 *Greater Delhi: A Study in Urbanization, 1940-1957.* Bombay: Asia Publishing House.

RAY, TALTON
1969 *The Politics of the Barrios of Venezuela.* Berkeley and Los Angeles: University of California Press.

RAYMAEKERS, PAUL
1964 *L'Organisation des zones de squatting.* Paris: Editions universitaires.

REDFIELD, ROBERT
1930 *Tepoztlán—A Mexican Village.* Chicago: University of Chicago Press.
1947 "The Folk Society," *American Journal of Sociology*, LII (January), 293-308.
1960 *The Little Community.* Chicago: University of Chicago Press.

REMPEL, HENRY
1971 "The Determinants of Rural-to-Urban Labor Migration in Kenya." Mimeographed. Department of Economics, University of Manitoba.

ROBERTS, BRYAN
1970 "Urban Poverty and Political Behavior in Guatemala," *Human Organization*, XXI, 1.

ROSBERG, CARL G., JR., AND JOHN NOTTINGHAM
1966 *The Myth of "Mau Mau": Nationalism in Kenya.* Nairobi: East African Publishing House.

ROSS, MARC HOWARD
1968 "Politics and Urbanization: Two Communities in Nairobi." Ph.D. dissertation, Northwestern University.
1973 "Two Styles of Political Participation in an African City," *Midwest Journal of Political Science*, XVII (February).

Forthcoming   *Grassroots in an African City: Political Behavior in Nairobi.*

SAFA, HELEN ICKEN
1968 "The Social Isolation of the Urban Poor: Life in a Puerto Rican Shanty Town." In *Among the People*, edited by Irwin Deutscher and Elizabeth J. Thompson,, pp. 335-51. New York: Basic Books.

SCHMITTER, PHILIPPE C.
1969 "Three Neo-Functionalist Hypotheses about International Integration," *International Organization*, XXIII, no. 1 (Winter), 161-66.
1970 "A Revised Theory of Regional Integration." In *Regional Integration: Theory and Research*, edited by Leon N. Lindberg and Stuart Scheingold. Cambridge: Harvard University Press.

SEGAL, EDWIN S.
1970 "The Cultural Background of East African Urban Migrants," *African Urban Notes*, V, 4.

SEN, S. N.
1960 *The City of Calcutta: A SocioEconomic Survey, 1954-1955 to 1957-1958.* Calcutta: Bookland Private Ltd.

SEWELL, G. H.
1964 *Squatter Settlements in Turkey: Analysis of a Social, Political and Economic Problem.* Ph.D. dissertation, Massachusetts Institute of Technology.

SIMMONS, LEO W.
1963 *Sun Chief: The Autobiography of a Hopi Indian.* New Haven, Conn.: Yale University Press.

SORRENSON, M. P. K.
1967 *Land Reform in Kikuyu Country.* Nairobi: Oxford University Press.

SOUTHALL, AIDAN
1960 "Introductory Summary." In *Social Change in Modern Africa*, edited by Aidan Southall, pp. 1-66. London: Oxford University Press.

SPIRO, MELFORD E.

1963 *Kibbutz.* New York: Schocken Books.

SUTTLES, GERALD

1968 *The Social Order of the Slum.* Chicago: University of Chicago Press.

TURNER, JOHN C.

1968a "Uncontrolled Urban Settlement: Problems and Policies," *International Social Development Review,* 1, UN(ST/SOA/SER.X/1), 107-30.

1968b "Housing Priorities, Settlement Patterns, and Urban Development in Modernizing Countries," *American Institute of Planners Journal* (November), pp. 354-63.

1968c "The Squatter Settlement: Architecture That Works,'.' *Architectural Design,* XXXVIII, no. 8 (August), 355-60.

1970 "Barriers and Channels for Housing Development in Modernizing Countries." In *Peasants in Cities,* edited by William P. Mangin. Boston: Houghton Mifflin.

TURNER, ROY, ED.

1962 *India's Urban Future.* Berkeley and Los Angeles: University of California Press.

VAN DER KROEF, JUSTUS MARIA

1954 *Indonesia in the Modern World.* Bandung: Masa Baru.

VAN HOEY, LEO

1968 "The Coercive Process of Urbanization: The Case of Niger." In *The New Urbanization,* edited by Scott Greer et al. New York: St. Martin's Press.

VERBA, SIDNEY

1961 *Small Groups and Political Behavior.* Princeton, N.J.: Princeton University Press.

VERSHUYS, J. D. N.

1964 "Urbanization in South-East Asia." In *Urbanism and Urbanization,* edited by Nels Anderson. Leiden, Netherlands: E. J. Brill.

VIDICH, ARTHUR, AND JOSEPH BENSMAN

1960 *Small Town in Mass Society.* Garden City, N.Y.: Doubleday Anchor.

Bibliography

WEST BENGAL STATE STATISTICAL BUREAU
1964 *Report on the Bustee Survey in Calcutta, 1958-59.* Consolidated Report, Vol. XVII. Alipore, West Bengal: West Bengal Government Press.

WHITEHEAD, ANDREW
1964 *Two Cities in Latin America.* Garden City, N.Y.: Doubleday Anchor.

WHYTE, WILLIAM F.
1966 *Street Corner Society.* Chicago: University of Chicago Press.

WILSON, GODFREY, AND MONICA WILSON
1965 *The Analysis of Social Change.* Cambridge: Cambridge University Press.

WIRTH, LOUIS
1938 "Urbanism as a Way of Life," *American Journal of Sociology,* XLIV, 1-24.

WOLFF, HANS
1964 "Intelligibility and Inter-Ethnic Attitudes." In *Language in Culture and Society,* edited by Dell Hymes. New York: Harper and Row.

YOUNG, MICHAEL, AND PETER WILLMOTT
1957 *Family and Kinship in East London.* London: Routledge and Kegan Paul.

INDEX

Abrams, Charles, 48
Almond, Gabriel, 5
Autonomy: of communities, 26,
  165; effect on integration, 80-81;
  of Mathare, 14, 89, 186-89, 200

Bales, Robert F., 79
Bancroft, Dick, 102
Becker, Howard, 146
Bensman, Joseph, 165
Bogue, Donald J., 45

Campbell, Angus, 5
Chambers, Robert, 27
Cobb, Roger, 150, 182 n
Community: concept of, 13, 22-27,
  36-37, 190-92; definition of, 22;
  formation of, 13, 20-37, 198-206;
  perceived importance of, 75-76,
  132-46, 154, 193-94, 200; size of,
  80, 184-86, 188, 197-98, 200;
  symbols of, 76-77, 202, 203. See
  also sense of community
Cooperative society, in Mathare, 7,
  8-9, 10, 102, 112, 202, 204, 209
Cornelius, Wayne, 71
Coser, Louis, 152

Danielski, David J., 79
Davis, Kingsley, 38
Deutsch, Karl, 27-28, 29, 33, 34,
  36, 98, 157, 164, 168
Dispute settlement. See Mathare
  Valley village 2: dispute
  settlement in
Doughty, Paul L., 46

Dwyer, D. J., 4, 49

Easton, David, 29-30
Edelman, Murray, 17, 34, 150
Effectiveness, of community
  institutions, 34, 69, 70, 78, 130,
  196
Elder, Charles D., 150, 182 n
Elders, committee of: cases heard
  by, 113-21; enforcement of
  decisions by, 122-23, 130; in
  Mathare, 7, 129-30
Epstein, A. L., 32, 33 n, 120, 183
Ethnicity, 15, 17, 160-62
Evans-Pritchard, E. E., 31

Fallers, Lloyd, 32
Frankenberg, Ronald, 24

Gachukia, W. Gitau, 8, 171, 197,
  209
Gans, Herbert, 26, 27, 191, 192
Gichohi, Kariuki, 103, 113, 115,
  171, 197
Gluckman, Max, 31, 152, 183
Goldrich, Daniel, 70, 71
Gordon, Milton, 15
Greer, Scott, 24, 38, 153 n, 184
Guetzkow, Harold, 26
Guha, Uma, 67

Haas, Ernst, 27, 34, 168
Hake, Andrew, 8, 11
Harbeson, John W., 16
Hellmann, Ellen, 68
Hillery, George A., Jr., 24, 26

225

Homer, Elizabeth L., 65, 66, 69 n
Homogeneity, cultural and social,
78; in Mathare, 155-64, 195-96,
200

Institutional generalizability, 79,
167-69, 196, 200, 202, 203; *See
also* spillover
Institutions and practices: in
Mathare, 155-81, 203; measures
of strength of, 125, 128-30;
strength of, 33-36, 77-80, 97-99
Interdependence: in communities,
24, 78; in Mathare, 89, 166-67,
202
Isolation, 80-81, 165. *See also*
autonomy

Jacob, Phillip, 27, 156
Johnson, Willard, 27

KANU Mathare, 7, 108, 111-12
Kenya: politics in, 14-18; State of
Emergency in, 6, 9, 16, 89, 90,
151, 201
Kenyatta, President Jomo, 16, 17,
101, 102, 150, 151, 195
Kershaw, Greet, 123, 186
Kiboro, E. W., 9, 10, 100, 101, 102,
103, 104, 109, 111, 129 n, 169,
171-72, 175-78, 179, 187, 196,
197, 209
Kikuyu, 15-16, 17, 89, 123, 150,
151, 160, 161, 185-86
Kinship: as a basis for integration,
24; in squatter settlements, 68;
See also Mathare Valley Village
2, household and family structure
in
Knoop, Henri, 66 n

Lambert, H. E., 123, 186
Leadership: selection in Mathare 2,
172; skills, 79-80; skills, in
Mathare, 7, 103, 169-79, 196-97,
200, 202, 204; in squatter
settlements, 50, 55
Lee, Terrence, 186
Leeds, Anthony, 44
Leeds, Elizabeth, 44

Léopoldville (Kinshasa), squatting
in, 49, 51-2, 66, 67, 71
Leys, Colin, 15
Lindberg, Leon, 27, 35
Little, Kenneth, 46
Luo, 15, 156

McGee, T. G., 65, 66, 68
McVicar, Kenneth, 87 n
Mangin, William, 4, 46, 51, 55, 60,
65, 67, 68, 69, 70, 71, 159, 162 n,
207
Mathare Valley Village 2: beer
brewing and selling, 6, 7, 12, 91,
105, 107-8, 136-39, 167, 202;
community organizations and
projects, 99-113; description of,
5-8, dispute settlement in,
113-24; economy of, 133-46;
employment in, 90-91, 96, 127,
135; finances in, 9, 12, 106, 111,
112, 127, 197; future of, 206-9;
household and family structure
in, 162-64; interaction patterns in,
164-66; location and settlement
of, 89-92; participation in, 100,
152-53, 154; police, 6, 7, 11-12,
102, 147-50, 177-78; political
integration, measures of, in,
124-31; renting rooms in, 140-41;
small-scale agriculture in, 143-44;
small shops and petty trade in,
141-43; social background of
residents in, 135-36; symbols of,
150-51, 154; threats to, 92, 94,
137, 146-50, 154, 194-95, 202;
water project in, 109-11, 202; *See
also* cooperative society; elders;
KANU Mathare; nursery school;
social hall; village committee; and
youth wing
Mboya, Tom, 15 n, 86 n
Merritt, Richard L., 98
Middleton, John, 123, 186
Migration: experience in Mathare,
83, 157-59; experience of
squatters, 65-66; in developing
countries, 40-45
Milbrath, Lester, 5
Minar, David, 24

Mitrany, David, 34
Morse, Richard, 45 n, 71, 72

Nairobi, 5, 82-92: attitudes about,
84-86; city council, 10, 11, 89, 90,
92, 94, 110; eviction of squatters,
52; racial divisions in, 82-83;
residential zones, 87-89; urban
growth in, 82-84
Naroll, Raoul, 124
Nelson, Joan, 16 n, 40, 60 n, 63
Neofunctionalism, 35, 98, 201
Nisbet, Robert, 22
Nottingham, John, 16
Nursery school, in Mathare, 7, 102,
103, 108-9, 201, 202
Nye, Joseph S., 35, 97, 99, 127, 168

Parker, Mary, 82, 87
Parkin, David, 156
Participation: in Mathare 100,
152-53, 154, 202, 203; in squatter
communities, 77
Patterson, Mary Jane, 8
Pearse, Andrew, 68
Perlman, Janice, 60 n
Political integration: concept of, 13,
27-37; definition of, 27-28; and
dispute settlement, 123-34; at the
local level, 182-89; in Mathare 2,
97-131, 192-98; measured in
Mathare, 124-31; in squatter
settlements, 73-81
Pons, Valdo, 187
Portes, Alejandro, 54, 65
Powell, Sandra, 71

Ray, Talton, 48, 50, 52, 61, 66, 68,
69, 70, 71, 72, 73, 74, 78, 81
Raymaekers, Paul, 49, 52, 66, 67, 71
Redfield, Robert, 26, 187
Rempel, Henry, 134 n
Rogler, L. H., 71
Rosberg, Carl G., Jr., 16
Ross, Marc Howard, 14, 15, 84, 85,
134 n

Scale, theory of increasing, 38
Scheingold, Stuart, 35
Schmitter, Phillippe E., 35, 36

Segal, Edwin S., 45 n
Sense of community, 28-33, 75, 77,
97-99; in Mathare, 8, 13, 132-54,
201, 203; measure of, 125-28
Sewell, G. H., 72
Simmons, Leo W., 33
Site-and-service schemes, in
Nairobi, 47, 93-94, 96, 207
Social hall, in Mathare, 7, 9, 12,
102, 103, 104, 105-8, 121, 122,
129, 202, 204
Sorrenson, M. P. K., 16
Spillover, 30, 36, 79, 167-69, 196.
See also institutional
generalizability
Spiro, Melford, 26, 205
Squatters: in Asian cities, 48-49; in
developing countries, 3-4, 45-62,
206-9; employment of, 66-67;
kinship ties of, 68; in Latin
American cities, 48, 49, 63-64,
206-7; migration experience of,
65-66
Squatter settlements: community
organization in, 69-72;
developmental patterns of, 53-61;
formation of, 49-53;
governmental assistance to, 61,
69-70; in Nairobi, 88-89; political
integration of, 73-81; social
disorganization in, 67-69; threats
to, 70-71, 76
Suttles, Gerald, 68, 187

Task expansion. *See* institutional
generalizability; spillover
Teune, Henry, 27, 156
Turner, John, 4, 49, 51, 53-61, 62,
66 n, 68, 70, 71, 72, 76, 78, 81,
146, 206, 207

Urbanization: in developing nations,
3-5, 38-45; pull factors in, 40-43;
push factors in, 40-42; as urban
commitment in Nairobi, 86-87;
urban growth, 38, 40-45

van Hoey, Leo, 38, 165
Verba, Sidney, 5, 152
Vidich, Arthur, 165

227

Village Committee, in Mathare, 7-9,
100-105, 201
Village meetings (*baraza*), in
Mathare, 10, 100-103, 111
Voluntary associations, in cities, 46

Waiyaki, Dr. Munyua, 108, 189
Whyte, William F., 68, 186
Willmott, Peter, 24

Wilson, Godfrey, 38, 165
Wilson, Monica, 38, 165
Wirth, Louis, 133

Young, Michael, 24
Youth wing, in Mathare, 7, 102,
103, 104, 105, 112-13, 115

Zachariah, K. C., 45